SOMETHING
Wonderful

The Journey of Hope Along Life's Way

KIM EDGE

Copyright © 2016 by Kim Edge

Something Wonderful
The Journey of Hope Along Life's Way
by Kim Edge

Printed in the United States of America.

Edited by Xulon Press.

ISBN 9781498474344

All rights reserved solely by the author. The author guarantees all contents are original and do not infringe upon the legal rights of any other person or work. No part of this book may be reproduced in any form without the permission of the author. The views expressed in this book are not necessarily those of the publisher.

Unless otherwise indicated, Scripture quotations taken from the Amplified Bible (AMPC). Copyright © 1967, 1987 by The Lockman Foundation. Used by permission. All rights reserved.

Scripture quotations taken from the King James Version (KJV) – *public domain*.

Scripture quotations taken from the New American Standard Bible (NASB). Copyright © 1960, 1962, 1963, 1968, 1971, 1972, 1973, 1975, 1977, 1995 by The Lockman Foundation. Used by permission. All rights reserved.

Scripture quotations taken from the Holy Bible, New International Version (NIV). Copyright © 1973, 1978, 1984, 2011 by Biblica, Inc.™. Used by permission. All rights reserved.

Scripture quotations taken from the New King James Version (NKJV). Copyright © 1982 by Thomas Nelson, Inc. Used by permission. All rights reserved.

Scripture quotations taken from the Holy Bible, New Living Translation (NLT). Copyright ©1996, 2004, 2007 by Tyndale House Foundation. Used by permission of Tyndale House Publishers, Inc.

www.xulonpress.com

For *Jesus*, Who rescued me from darkness and brought me into His marvelous Light. I look forward to eternity—to <u>worship You</u> and to <u>thank You</u>—because this lifetime could never be enough!

For Kelly Shane, the most fun, generous, loving husband a wife could ever have. Your *love for God* and *transformation in Him* amaze me daily. I'm thankful to be on this journey beside you!

For Kaleigh Brooke, the best daughter ever. Your life brought joy before you were even born. God has great things planned for you. Remember, you are *blessed* and *highly favored*!

For all my wonderful family and friends out there... Thank you for being you!

"For we are God's masterpiece.
He has created us anew in Christ Jesus,
so we can do the good things
he planned for us long ago."
(Ephesians 2:10, NLT)

Contents

Introduction..................................ix

Chapter 1:   Something About Transparency 13
Chapter 2:   Daddy's Girl 21
Chapter 3:   October Babies 29
Chapter 4:   Learning To Be a Sister.............. 43
Chapter 5:   Learning From My Sisters 55
Chapter 6:   The Prodigal and the Parent 69
Chapter 7:   Good Fruit........................ 87

Introduction

I remember the day I strolled through a Barnes and Noble, looking at all those books on the shelves. That was the day I decided I would *never* write a book—just to be left on some shelf in a bookstore, taking up space and collecting dust with all the rest. Yet here I sit, just typing away for this book to be published one day in the near future. I was content for over five years to write many daily posts on Facebook and journal in lots of different notebooks. Early on into social media I realized there was enough negativity in the world. If I were going to put something out there in cyberspace, it didn't need to add to the white noise, bad news, and constant complaints. It should have a purpose, even if mostly to make me think about my words and attitudes. (I can have some words and attitudes!)

I tried to push away the thought of writing something longer than a four-paragraph Facebook post or lengthy Instagram caption. Besides, who has time to write a book and hash up all the details of life and love and heartache and laughter? The idea wouldn't leave me, though. Through prayer—and simply not rushing into it, or delaying until I talked myself out of it—God began to make it clear *He would walk me through* it. The main things I needed to do were make sure my husband supported me (because of the time I would need to devote to writing), and check my motives.

As you can see, my sweet husband was for this, 150%. So why would I really do this, anyway? Well, I want our daughter to know some of the things I've made it through. There may be things she can relate to as she gets older and reads this with a mind of maturity. If this ends up in the hands of one person who can relate and is encouraged, or someone is strengthened in their faith, or if this could be another piece in the puzzle for someone wanting to know the *truth* about their purpose in life—it was well worth the investment.

The internet and social media have exploded, and there will be no turning back; but there's just something about diving into the depths of a book. This is a legacy that, most importantly, should express the *magnificent love* of our God for us. The lengths Jesus went through for us—from birth to death to resurrection and ascension—should be seen in the details of our life. It's simply a wonderful thing to remember and acknowledge that our heavenly Father is concerned with *every detail* of our lives.

In Ecclesiastes 3:11, we are told that God has planted eternity in our human hearts. We have a built-in longing for the *extra*-ordinary, a craving for the *super*-natural. Every love

Introduction

story in print or cinema speaks of the desire to love, and to be loved. Every song that grips you and every adventure that moves you is inspired by these desires of your *heart*.

We're each on a journey, learning to love, to live, and to be fruitful. As Paul prayed for the people of long ago, may this prayer also be for us today: "I pray that God, the source of *hope*, will fill you completely with *joy* and *peace* because you *trust* in him. *Then* you will overflow with *confident hope* through the *power* of the *Holy Spirit*." (Romans 15:13, NLT, emphasis added)

May you be blessed as you read this, and may you see God at work as He unfolds His Truth and Love into your heart, soul, and spirit.

Chapter One
Something about Transparency

It's a good thing to remember that our heavenly Father is concerned with *every detail* of our lives. Oh man, what a battle I went through to say, "Okay, I'll begin writing a book." I came up with lots of excuses; I didn't have time, or creativity, or the energy for it. Have you noticed that most of the battles we fight are internal? Sure, someone may hear us blow up, or see us explode when we've reached our boiling point. Although for the most part, our internal dialogue *is* what makes us or breaks us. Hi, I'm Kim. Welcome to my world, and the battles I've chosen with stubbornness, pride, and being a self-proclaimed rebel and "deep thinker." Of course, those chosen battles started with an untamed thought life. And so, the journey unfolds…

There was a blog I once found saying every person has at least one good book in them. I suppose that's true. We definitely all have a story. Even if we don't think it's a very good one, we also have a testimony. For many, it's the story of their tests and trials; for others, it's facing the truth about themselves. So what could make this rebellious, set-in-her-ways gal begin such an undertaking? It's simple. *I've fallen in love.* Don't start thinking I'm being all mushy about my husband. Yes, we've been married over ten years, and I totally adore him. I'm speaking of a love I never knew existed back when I had those first butterflies for Kelly Edge. This **finding true love** journey started way before I knew there was such a thing.

I was painfully shy as a girl growing up. There always seemed to be this vague sense that everyone around knew what was going on; I just floated through, not knowing what was really happening. Although there was a lot of comfort in routine and tradition, things got shaken up a lot when there were changes. This could be when a new school year was approaching, when it was time to pack and move (because any house we lived in was always for sale since my father is a homebuilder; we moved twice a year on average), and when things just didn't go like they were "supposed to."

If you've ever dealt with people, a big, red flag should go up now. Just stay in relationship with someone long enough, and things won't go as you planned. You will even surprise yourself sometimes with the things you think or hear spoken out of your own mouth. Needless to say, if you've been alive on this planet for any length of time, you have encountered setbacks and disappointments, heartache and frustration. You may have gone through terribly painful circumstances up to this point—through your choices, from other people's choices, or just as life happened. Some of you will even say, "My childhood was good, with lots of happy memories, but it seems like there should be more to life now...now that I'm 'grown up' and living the American dream."

I am here to encourage you and say there IS more, there IS a greater love, there IS more purpose and passion for your life than you could have ever imagined! This is coming from that shy little girl who looked around years ago—like so many people do—and we wonder: is there more than what my eyes can see, am I really something special, am I loved, and what about this big love I have on the inside to give away??

You see, that timid, insecure girl began a journey of searching for the *more* in life. Any confidence I could muster up went into relationships with friends; how I thought they perceived me seemed so important. I got value from being an honor roll student and doing things "by the books" until I was 15 and began underage drinking. That soon led to getting self-worth from guys and added to a lifestyle of dysfunction. Everything eventually came up short.

Drinking, depression, drug use, and a suicide attempt are part of my story. BUT GOD...! He has been *so* merciful and loving to give me each and every day since those dark times. Yes, dear reader, that's who I used to be, but I'd like to introduce you to the new Kim. I have been so radically affected by the Love of God that I now look for *good things* in life, instead of expecting the worst. I can't be quiet about what He has done (and what He continues to do) in my life!

We all have details. I want to take you on this journey with me, and at least get you to the path where you find the steps for yourself. Or, you may be at a place where you bear witness with what I share of my journey so far. We can celebrate together! You may have found this incredible Love, but your heart aches for those around you who seem to be willfully and belligerently running in the opposite direction. We can cry together. Wherever you are at this moment is no surprise to God. The point is, don't stay there.

If you need to get your heart right with God, today is the day for your salvation! If you have unforgiveness and bitterness, ask God to help you truly forgive, and *trust Him more* than you trust your feelings. If God is calling you higher to walk in love and unity with His children, move past denominational barriers and people-differences; see the Body of Christ at large on the planet today. We are the formidable army that will carry the Good News to the ends of the earth!

The main message for each of our lives is **Love**. It's what we really want and search for, but often look for in all the wrong places. God's love is the only real *hope* we have for Life and Joy and Peace. There *is* something about transparency that helps others **see**—and helps you be **free**. I am painfully aware of my weaknesses and shortcomings, yet it is amazing how God can shine through even our pitifully cracked vessels. Our God is the only One Who can love us completely and restore us to wholeness.

I am much more careful these days with what I *proclaim about myself* (the rebel in me has become a rebel for Jesus, and a self-proclaimed Jesus freak) and what I *declare about the Lord* (He is my Refuge and my Place of Safety, He is my God and I trust Him, He is my Stability in a very unstable world). He has such sweet ways to guide and teach us, and bittersweet ways to discipline and prune us. Salvation came to my soul one day, and the journey has been nothing short of amazing. The Love of Jesus has so totally transformed my heart and mind that I'm like a new person. Oh, you should have seen my excitement when I found and read 2 Corinthians 5:17, which says,

"This means that anyone who belongs to Christ has become a new person. The old life is gone; a new life has begun!" (NLT)

Let's get to first things first in this opening chapter. If you've put it off... If you can't really pinpoint a time you gave your heart to Jesus... If you had a moving experience once or twice, but never really changed your ways... then God may be calling you into a relationship with Him. It is not about a weekly church routine. It is not goose bumps that fizzle out by mid-week. The Creator of everything you can see and cannot see wants to help you in life! He wants to love you into wholeness. If a person gave his life for you and you could thank him, wouldn't you want to? Since Jesus *did* give His life for you, don't you want to know Him better? If this is your heart, you can begin your journey today...

Prayer Starter:

Dear Father, I am so sorry for choosing a lifestyle of sin over You. I ask You to please forgive me. I believe You sent Jesus to pay the price for my sins, which I could never ever pay for myself. I believe Jesus died on the cross and was resurrected on the third day. You have made the Way for me through Jesus. God, I receive Your precious gift of salvation so I can be reconciled to You. I accept Jesus as my Savior and as my Lord. I give You all that I am, and all that I'm not. I trust You to make me who You've created me to be. I believe I'm born again, and I will be joined with You for eternity after my last breath on this earth. Thank You, God, for saving me! In Jesus' Name! Amen!!

It's just like that! "If you openly declare that Jesus is Lord and believe in your heart that God raised Him from the dead, you will be saved." (Romans 10:9, NLT) On February 22, 2009, I opened my heart fully to Jesus. Now the old Kim is gone, and the new Kim has found Life in Jesus. You need to declare it, too. Go ahead, out loud, and put your name in there: "The old _____ is gone, and the new _____ has found Life in Jesus." Amen!

Chapter Two

Daddy's Girl

I've always been a Daddy's girl. Even if I call him up today, he'll say, "Hi Baby." Sometimes I hear people say they wish they could talk to their mom or dad just one more time. That always makes me want to call them. Ummm, I'll be right back...I need to call my Daddy......(7 minutes later) Yep: "Hi Baby!" That makes me smile big every time. :)

I'm so thankful for the parents I have. They've been married over 46 years, and are *so cute* together. I know they had struggles and the same difficulties every couple has when trying to raise a family, balance work and fun, and keep their sanity through the ups and downs of life. Growing up, I never heard them argue about money or fight about grown up things. What I do remember, and is something that I still cherish today, was when we'd sit down for dinner and they would talk about their day. There were some matter-of-fact conversations and lots of laughter spread throughout those family meals.

Many of the mealtimes were at favorite restaurants, since Mama worked and it was easier to go out a few nights a week than cook and clean after a full day. My younger sister, Leigh Ann (who you will see lovingly referred to as Baby Sister), and I occasionally talk about the pleasant times we remember from childhood. We don't remember much at all about the food we ate; we remember laughter, and we remember sharing about the day and simply being together. It was a time of comfort and a place where we were safe. There's something very special about family, and about peace that has the potential to blossom inside a well-nurtured home. This is something I want to pass on to my daughter.

Living in a home with your family exposes everyone's shortcomings and weaknesses, but what a place to extend mercy! What great lessons are learned from living in close, close community with family. It's really true that blood is thicker than water. There's this bond that can make family survive the seemingly un-survivable. It is having (and making *on purpose*) more of the happy memories to outweigh the bad ones. It's also having an attitude of peace and overall kindness when dealing with daily "stuff." The stuff could be "Is all your homework done?" or "What's for dinner tonight?" or "I thought *you* would take out the garbage before it started stinking up the house!" We all have lots of stuff go on at home. I believe home should be a sanctuary from the world, a place to rest and take refuge, and enjoy those around you.

Regardless of how your childhood was—like "Leave it to Beaver" or "It Left Me Messed Up"—your family life *now* can be what *you* decide you want it to be. You may say, "My husband drinks too much and I can't help but blow up at him in front of the kids." Dear friend, you need Jesus to give you the stability your family desperately needs to see lived out. Your husband may be doing what he saw his dad doing, or he doesn't know any other way to unwind from the stress in life. He may be running from change, or just flat out selfish. But you...you can dig into the Word of God and pull out life-saving verses that get you through the toughest of days, and the most difficult of moments.

Instead of saying you can't go on like this, or it's just too hard for you, say, "I can do all things through Christ who strengthens me." (Philippians 4:13, NKJV) Those words coming out of *your mouth*, heard by *your ears*, strengthening *your* hurting heart, are more powerful than those self-defeating words. *Get in agreement with God.* He so dearly loves you! He wants the best for you and your family, most definitely. Yet each of us has to make the decision for ourselves.

I'll go ahead and let you in on the key to transforming your home into the place your heart desires it to be: *change your thinking.* If you have lousy, stinkin' thinkin', it will eventually come out of your mouth. Even the attitude we walk around with is just our thought life turned inside out.

Whether we like it or not, we as women have great influence when setting the tone of our home. When you receive the love God wants to give so freely, when you get in agreement with God, and when you have a heartbeat for the things of God, you will begin to change the atmosphere of your space. This affects everywhere you are—your home, your car, your workplace, your classroom, in the stores where you shop, and so on.

A Shocking Love

I remember heading straight into a chaotic, out of balance place when Kelly and I married in 2005. That's because my mind and thoughts were so chaotic and out of balance. This leads into sharing more transparency, then freedom...

After my first marriage ended in my mid-20's, I felt like a complete failure. Never did I think I'd be labeled a "divorcee." Weekend drinking with some friends turned into several years of binges and full-blown sin. When I met Kelly and the Pickwick party crowd, there were fast boats and hard drugs. Using alcohol as a numbing tool made it easy to start the array of recreational drugs available with my new friends. A few weeks before I turned 30, things were inevitably about to crash and burn.

As you might expect, things were strained between Kelly and me. One day, after he would not go home or answer my calls, I went to his house and took as many pills as I could find. I got to a friend's house before they kicked in, and she had the hard job of calling my mom to say something was terribly wrong. I ended up in ICU on a ventilator. They had to shock my heart back to life several times. I know I survived for a reason. There is purpose for my living through that suicide attempt. A glimmer of hope was faint at best, but it was there.

It's so surreal to describe now—like a bad dream or a book I read about someone else. It is not even that I wanted to die. (There had been times of intense depression on and off for 15 years—half my life up until that point.) I just remember wanting the pain to stop. Making myself numb to the reality in this life never really worked. The hopelessness that engulfed me was all-consuming; never had the darkness been so real. I didn't know how to stop the constant ache from my lifestyle of addiction and more rejection from someone I loved.

A year went by, and I wanted to learn how to be loved and to love someone. For months, I hoped to marry Kelly, while my mind was trying to heal and "find its place." He seemed to be so slow to commit. We were on a boat ride when Kelly got on one knee and proposed; I was elated, but was still on dangerous ground.

The weekend we were engaged, I began using cocaine again. It was a lie straight out of hell to think it would "help me" to be more fun, sociable, and relaxed. There was an ominous, pervasive undertone of depression. It stemmed from those melancholy moods of my teenage years. I also continued with the antidepressants I started in my 20's. There seemed such a fog of unhappiness, while—from the outside looking in—all should have been really good.

There's not an easy way to describe the very real darkness of depression. It was like being in a tunnel—and I should see light at the end of it—but there was only heaviness and deep sadness. I had no idea at the time this could be a spiritual matter—*a matter of the heart*. I became good at blending in where I needed to be and with whom I was around. For years, to gear up for a crowd and being around people, I found myself using alcohol. Did I actually ever think that was fun?!

The first time I drank was a sneaky, pleasant buzz. I knew it was wrong. (After that, guilt was a constant covering, lasting for years.) The next time, I was puking stomach acid out my nose. Alcohol was the gateway drug that led to using cocaine, ecstasy, hydros (pills), marijuana, and the antidepressant of the month. As you can imagine, this didn't make for a stable, well-rounded person. My life was spiraling out of control. Although I never really was in control, the hopeless state of my existence called for answers; even more, it demanded I make a choice. You know what? It's hard to give an answer when you're not even sure what the question should be. Everything was culminating into the looming question: would I choose Life, or death?

For years, I unknowingly handed all power and authority over to the enemy of ours. Back then, I didn't know what 1

Peter 5:8 says: "Be well balanced (temperate, sober of mind), be vigilant *and* cautious at all times; for that enemy of yours, the devil, roams around like a lion roaring [in fierce hunger], seeking someone to seize upon *and* devour." (AMPC) I am *forever grateful* at how God so sweetly began to pull me from the clutches of the devil and draw me to Himself. *There is no power on this earth that compares to the great love of our God!*

When faced with the reality of who I was and the filth of my sin, it's nothing short of shocking that our God would love me—an especially wicked sinner and enemy of His. Even in the years of my good-girl days, I was an enemy of the cross simply because I was living for me and not for Him. Oh, my goodness! Oh, what a love!

It's because of God's wonderful love that I am now *His girl*…and I know something intrinsically about being a Daddy's Girl. I know it makes me special—not because I do everything right and in the right timing—but because *I am His*.

Chapter Three

October Babies

It was March of 2006. I packed my bag to head to Nashville, and was going to see my Baby Sister. She would be on bed rest for several more months until she had her baby boy, Brody. Kelly and I had gone together to stay with Leigh Ann and Epp, but while he was hunting I would go and stay a few days here and there. I would go and take my supply of drugs. One time, I almost ran out and abruptly packed up and left to go home—just so I could get my next fix. No one knew the cycle of addiction I was in so deeply, but they probably knew something wasn't right. Isn't that how it usually is? You can tell if something's not quite right, even if you can't pinpoint it.

On February 2, before this trip, Kelly and I had partied it up on our one-year anniversary. We took our boat down the river from Pickwick Lake and locked through several dams. Sad to say, it was kind of a blur—like many memories over those years. (That may also be a blessing for these days.) We grilled steaks and feasted on Kelly's good cooking. We drank and got high, and thought we were living the life. When we got home, we went straight into Super Bowl party mode.

I ran out of cocaine and money after our anniversary blowout. Kelly went back to Arkansas to live in the duck blinds a few more weeks, or maybe he was scouting for deer somewhere. I had scoured all of his hiding places, "fiending" (as I call that addiction craving) for whatever I could find; but the drugs couldn't be found, and I was a mess trying to carry on with life as normal. When he came back home a couple of times in February, I just didn't want to go to the good ole boys hangout, watching NASCAR and smelling cigarettes and beer. I pretty much wanted to nap on the couch on Sunday afternoons that month. When March came around and fishing season was next, here I was headed to Nashville with some big plans.

I decided I would tan, buy some diet pills, and I was going to buy a Corvette. I literally laughed out loud just now, but those were my plans. I often retaliated against my husband when he left to hunt by spending money we really didn't have; it was my way of saying, "I'll show you!" He never mentioned the spending; we were so dysfunctional then, he didn't want to rock the boat and be asked about what *he* was spending time and money on.

Baby Sister was in her last trimester and on bed rest, so I went to the grocery store and bought cookie dough and fruit— lots of fruit. I never got around to tanning; I was much happier baking chocolate chip cookies and cutting the kiwi and strawberries than thinking about some type of diet. I only drove past the car lots as I flew down the interstate, so I barely got a quick sweep of the Corvette inventory. I remember having a backache, and thought I needed a heating pad. I probably took some Midol®, because it was about that time of the month. I even made sure I had some tampons and pads, because that's just what a woman has to do. Baby Sister and I enjoyed our time together in Nashville, watching On-Demand® TV, eating fruit and baking cookies.

When I got home, Kelly was in full-on sauger fishing mode. Fishing is something I really like to do with Kelly. He is so good to bait my hook and take off the fish I catch. That leaves me with the exciting part of reeling all those fish in — the sauger, stripers, crappie, bream, bass, catfish, drums, etc. I've always been thankful he doesn't mind doing that for me. Especially since I am so very tenderhearted towards animals and don't like to see or hear the "sad" details of hunting down and killing. I've gotten to where I at least show interest by asking if he got one or some (depending on what he's after) and he has learned to give me the short answer with no details that would make me cry. Fishing, however, has always been some common ground for us.

Kelly and his dad were scheduled to fish the March sauger tournament in Savannah. I was in bed, not feeling the perkiest when Kelly's mom called to ask if I was going to join the guys at Savannah Bridge for the weigh-in and fish cooking.

I explained that I didn't feel much like going. I had this kind of queasy, blah feeling and was going to stay around the house. She was fine with that, and needed to work around home anyway. I lay back down in bed, and the clearest things began to unwrap in my thoughts: I felt queasy...could it be called a little nausea? I had unusually bad back pain at Baby Sister's...but not really a full blown period, right? A-HA!!! Could I be pregnant?!?

I jumped up, got dressed, and went to Fred's to buy 3 or 4 boxes of pregnancy tests. Oh my word, YES!!! I was going to be a mother! *Something changed in that instant.* I never remember being drawn to God (at least since a young teenager) like that moment began to draw me. It was all very subtle at first, but something in me was so gripped because I was no longer only responsible for myself. Suddenly, there was meaning past the here and now.

I waited what seemed like hours and hours for Kelly to get home, and peed on a few more sticks. When he walked in, I met him at the door. I said I wanted to show him something, but he wanted time to shower and put fresh clothes on. I waited for him to finish; he seemed to move in slow motion to get dressed, but finally I had his attention. I ushered him into the other bathroom where the first pregnancy test was blaring (+) POSITIVE. Oh my, again!!! He was so excited and wanted to know if I was for sure, so I showed him the other tests I had done and yet another one I could do right then so he could see. I don't think we did another test right away, because he was back in the living room looking for his phone to call his mom. I said, "Wait, I haven't even told my Mama yet!" So I called my parents as he called his, and our journey was set before us that day.

Preparing for New Life

I wish I could say my pregnancy and path to becoming a mother and better wife was a smooth one, but it was anything but that. Now remember, I had only run out of drugs weeks before finding out I was pregnant. My body was still going through all kinds of torment coming out of daily cocaine use, mixed with lots of alcohol and marijuana and some pills on the side. I began facing the reality that I didn't know what kind of harm I had done to our baby or my body. Daily, with much loneliness and isolation, I was the only one who knew the extent of all that. I worried about so much and experienced paralyzing fear about the unknown.

I was 33 years old, and my body seemed to go into shock while nurturing this new life that was growing inside me. I had every symptom you've ever heard of with pregnancy, and some you may have never heard of. For instance, I noticed big time what I called excessive salivation. When I walked Bailey and Harley (my two Boxers) outside, I would take a step and spit, take two more steps and spit. I mentioned it to my mom, who is a nurse, and she just said, "Hmmm." Sometime later she heard of another lady who had this symptom and actually took a spit cup around during her pregnancies. My bite changed when I chomped down my jaws, and my body felt like some foreign alien body I was trapped in. I also spotted quite a bit those first weeks, but was so relieved when we heard the first rapid, healthy heartbeats of our baby at the doctor's office in Tupelo, MS.

The first trimester was the hardest. I still have a notebook with questions/concerns/notes I took to ask Dr. Jack, who would deliver our baby. My notes were something like this...

- 1st visit: ask about swimming in lake water, natural sun light [I knew better than tanning beds!], ask about safety in getting my hair colored, exercise—what to do and not do, benefits of testing later for any problems [which was so scary for me because no one knew what I was just coming out of]
  —Get insurance/payment information
  —Pap Smear/Breast Exam
  —Sonogram= 108 bpm, .61 mm
  —6 weeks/3 days
  —Saw heart beat! (flash)
  —Drew blood
  —Dr. Jack Kahlstorf
     *goal, gain < 30 lbs.
     *spotting=off feet 24 hours then light activity
     48 hrs. no spotting=resume as normal

- 2nd visit: 2 huge problems affecting normal life
  1) Fatigue and nausea
  2) Lack of understanding from baby's father

SERIOUSLY?! Yes, seriously. I did write that in the notebook I carried back and forth to the doctor's office for all my checkups. Looking back, I remember the uncomfortable times of pregnancy. Another thing that made it so painfully difficult (especially the first trimester) was the underlying tension and distance that was eating away at our marriage.

Kelly would go to all the baby doctor visits with me, and even went to Preparation for Birth classes at the Women's Hospital with me. I tended to focus on the facts that Kelly was still drinking and occasionally partying with friends that would definitely have drugs around them. I focused on everything I thought he should be doing to help out or make my life easier. I seethed with quiet anger every time I carried all the groceries in by myself, each time I felt sick in the shower and thought I could just pass out and he'd never know because his head was stuck in the phone or watching TV, and when I couldn't get him to feel sorry for me and my discomfort.

I wanted things from him he had no idea how to give. I never told him what I expected or needed; I thought he was the man and should just know. Keep in mind, I never asked what *he* needed or what I could do to make *his* life easier. I was so busy judging his motives I barely could enjoy his company. Talk about dysfunction! That carried on terribly the first trimester, got a little better the second trimester (as I started physically feeling better), and went into the last trimester when my body was being pushed to its limits again with new life on the verge of being here.

Looking back at my notebook, here are some other things I wrote:

- 3rd visit: Took out belly ring, lost 1 lb., gained 3 lbs. so far, schedule a sonogram, baby's heart: 144-148, Dr. Jack said "It's a boy" if the old wives' tale is true=a boy's heart rate is under 150 and a girl's is over 150, in a couple of weeks I can feel the baby move!
- 4th visit: Saw four chambers of the heart, three veins in umbilical cord, good spine, stomach, and liver, all measurements looked good, *95% sure=It's a GIRL*, didn't see any boy parts/cord was in the way some.
- 5th visit: Feel good! Hands/feet started swelling this week (sitting hrs. at a time at work and the heat), start iron supplement, Colace if needed, lots of fiber and water.
- 6th visit: *Her* pulse was around 146/147, find out about 4D ultrasound next week (Friday, August 25th @ 11 a.m.), Find out about –crib mattress –humidifier – painting nursery –dog hair/dust in house –Dreft/special laundry detergent.
- 7th visit: Gained 4 more lbs., 20 lbs. total, *Kaleigh weighed 3 lbs., 14 oz.*, top of uterus measured 32 ½

weeks, 4D Ultrasound: eyes open, tinkled, hair on her head, Dr. Jack mentioned: back pain, feet swelling, indigestion=it's not unbearable (temporary) :)
- 8th visit: Gained 5 lbs., sharp pain very low, twitch/vibration below sternum, tired and more moody (like first trimester).
- 9th visit: Gained 5 more lbs., 30 lbs. so far, top of uterus has grown as far up as it can! Baby's heartbeat was pretty consistent at 150 bpm, swelling, joint discomfort all part of it, Dr. Jack said 26 days to go! Not dilated yet.
- 10th visit: Tuesday, October 10, 2006, no progression, gained 2 lbs.
- 11th visit: Tuesday, October 17, 2006, 50% effaced/1 cm dilated, lost 1 lb.
- 12th visit: Tuesday, October 24, **We'll induce Thursday!!!** Don't eat or drink after midnight Weds., be @ the hospital 6 a.m.

Learning to Push

Can you relate? If you've carried a child, those details may have stirred your memory some. Just maybe, there's a guy reading this who is close to someone who gave birth, but you can't physically relate to the changes in a woman's body during pregnancy. Sweet girl, maybe you are waiting for the right guy to come along before you even consider what it would be like during pregnancy. Or, you may be a mother who didn't give birth, but you love with your full heart as though you did. I want to stretch your thinking here just a little.

Whether you have carried a child or not, dear reader, you have most likely been pregnant with a dream or something you've envisioned coming to pass. You go through situations that stretch you (and have feelings that seem so foreign) when you pursue your passion and seek God whole-heartedly. You may pack on burdens like weight on a pregnant woman. Your baby must have nourishment, even while the weight gain causes swelling and discomfort. Just remember, your experiences (the trials you endure, and burdens you carry for things that are important to the heart of God) are building and giving nourishment to this birthing process within you.

There's a great story in the Bible about Abraham and Sarah. Although originally found in Genesis in the Old Testament, I want you to see what the writer of Hebrews, in chapter 11, has to say in the New Testament about their faith journey:

> "[8] [Urged on] by faith Abraham, when he was called, obeyed and went forth to a place which he was destined to receive as an inheritance; and he went, although he did not know *or* trouble his mind about where he was to go.
>
> [9] [Prompted] by faith he dwelt as a temporary resident in the land which was designated in

the promise [of God, though he was like a stranger] in a strange country, living in tents with Isaac and Jacob, fellow heirs with him of the same promise.

[10] For he was [waiting expectantly and confidently] looking forward to the city which has fixed *and* firm foundations, whose Architect *and* Builder is God.

[11] Because of faith also Sarah herself received physical power to conceive a child, even when she was long past the age for it, because she considered [God] Who had given her the promise to be reliable *and* trustworthy *and* true to His word." (AMPC)

That passage is so amazing every time I read it! By faith, Abraham, when called, set out on his journey. He was close enough to the heart of God that he heard the call, he obeyed, and he went...even though he didn't know where he was going! His name was Abram (meaning high, exalted father) when he set out in Genesis 12, and remained so until he was ninety-nine years old—when God changed it to Abraham (meaning father of a multitude). (See Genesis 17:1-5)

So often in life we don't really know where we're going. Anyone can have a good plan for a happy, successful life.

The ones who hear God calling soon realize we must have a *godly* plan for a *joyful* life. This comes from being right with God and obeying His Word. Some of the most painful things we go through are when God calls us out of a place where we have settled. This can be out of a relationship that is not healthy, out of routines of addiction, away from traditions and worldly pleasure, out of mediocrity; the purpose is to cut ties from those things that are slowly killing us.

We all learn to push in one way or another. I pushed against authority with a rebellious and prideful attitude. I pushed against peace with my husband because I wanted to be understood, without taking the time to understand. Something beautiful happened the instant I saw with my own eyes that I was going to have a baby. Just because that impacted me so deeply didn't mean my husband would break free from bondage in the same way. (It was just like when I'd visit my sister in Nashville when she first found out she was pregnant: I thought it would help stop my drug addiction, but I had to have my *own eyes* open to the truth of new life *in me*.)

I'm still learning to push, but these days it's learning to *push through*. We can learn to push through fear of the unknown by replacing fear with *faith*. When Hebrews 11:8 says Abraham "went, although he did not know *or* trouble his mind about where he was to go," (AMPC) I take that as a huge victory of faith over fear. He spent time with God. He knew God made a way when there seemed no way. It was not Abraham's job to trouble his mind about the journey. His part was to *be obedient* and *trust God*. Dear friends, this is our part as well.

I didn't grow up thinking I would turn into a drug addict. I never related that first drink of alcohol at age 15 to a downward spiral of depression, addiction, and darkness. Oh, but now, I celebrate life on my birthday every October; I celebrate my October baby, our beautiful, lovely, healthy child we named Kaleigh Brooke—who brought laughter, excitement, and love for life into our home. Those months I was pregnant were packed with so much growth. There were ups and downs, excitement and nervousness. At times, I just seemed an emotional mess. Other times were filled with a longing for *something more*, something deeper than just going through the motions in this world. God had caused a shaking in my life that would bring about pain and difficulties, but would equip me with a *heart to follow Him* with my all.

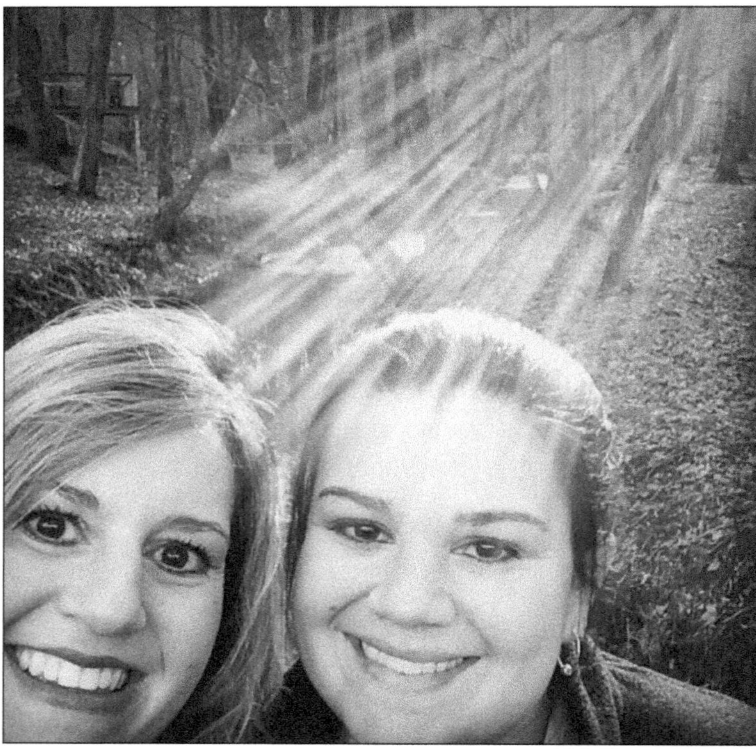

Chapter Four
Learning To Be a Sister

My sister, Leigh Ann, was born when I was five and a half years old. I don't exactly remember the details, but my father tells these stories of my first experiences with "Baby Sister." My parents were talking about names for her, and Daddy said he liked Leigh dash Ann. He was talking about a hyphen, like Leigh – Ann, but I blurted out, "I don't like the middle name Dash!" Another one of the funny stories I reportedly took part in was after they brought Baby Sister home. I let them know after a week I was ready to "take her back where they got her from."

It's funny to remember those first stories of becoming a sibling. Although I don't remember wanting to take her back, I do remember feeling like her caregiver and protector from an early age. I remember Leigh Ann bringing fun and laughter into our home. She was cute as a button and I wanted to always be there for her when she needed me. That has carried on over the years. I told her what I now tell KB (Kaleigh

Brooke), my baby girl: call me any time you need me, day or night, wherever you are, and I'll be there for you. Baby Sister has made those phone calls throughout the years. On one occasion, it was to pick her up from a bad situation. Mostly, it was to pour her heart out when she really needed to talk about something. There have been lots of times I gave her a call, too, just because I needed my Baby Sister.

Have you experienced how birth order can have a huge influence on personality? I was a pretty serious and responsible child. There were many things I put pressure on myself to make happen. Baby Sister was fun and more carefree; I really loved life around her. She brought balance into our home with lots of laughter and was not always taking things so seriously. Life as the oldest child can bring unforeseen pressure and responsibilities. I don't remember someone forcing me to aim for perfection, but it was a driving force in me for years.

The first time in elementary school I brought home an F on a paper, I locked myself in the bathroom crying. Mama finally got out of me why I was so upset. "I'm going to fail the third grade!" I belted out. I really believed failing one thing caused you to fail the entire year, and you would have to repeat it. My Pappaw Bryant rewarded me with $1 for every A and $.50 for every B on my report cards. I was never punished for bad grades, however, or told I better make good grades. I did want to please the teachers and adults in my life, and I took it all very seriously. I still have to be careful to remember that failing something doesn't mean I've failed life.

There is a definite correlation with birth order and some of the attributes we develop. My husband is the baby of the family. He is also fun-loving and would rather be laughing and having fun than weighed down with seriousness. I'm really thankful for the balance God brings into our lives with all our different personalities and characteristics. Imagine how boring or frightening things would be if everyone had your personality, or someone's personality who is the exact opposite of you. God is most definitely into variety; looking around at the myriad of birds, trees, flowers, fish, animals, stars, etc., gives a hint of His vastness, beauty, and care for detail.

You might look around at the people in your life and see exactly what I'm saying. Maybe a difficult person at work or school could be more easily understood if we took time to understand their family dynamic, their insecurities, their need to please, even their having been babied for years and years, or, their lack of purpose and identity. We want God to accept us as we are, so we must often give others the same grace we have received. The wonderful thing with God is that He doesn't leave us there; He molds, shapes, and prunes us into our best—for His glory *and* our good.

We do ourselves a huge favor when we take others off the potter's wheel. God, Who draws men, women, boys, and girls to Himself, is the One with all the information—not us. We can trust that He *will* work and *is* working in the lives of those around us. As a sister, a friend, even an acquaintance, you have insight to pray specifics for the people in your life. Sometimes with the most hardened or selfish hearts, your prayer can simply be, "Lord, please open their eyes and soften their hearts. Don't let them be deceived."

Polar Opposites

Some of your closest friends very likely have the same interests, hobbies, or beliefs as you. What about this: do opposites really attract? We think of people marrying their opposite and quickly drawing the conclusion that they're "not compatible." I'll take it a step further. Who in this world really *is* compatible? Sure, we may have the love-struck butterflies—and be sickeningly smitten—for a while. At some point, the honeymoon is always over. Once again, here we are, back at *love*. At its greatest, love is a choice and not a feeling. It's the decision not to be rude, touchy, resentful, and insisting its own way. It's not being boastful, envious, or jealous. *Love* endures a lot—while being patient, kind, and believing the best about people. We hear a lot about faith, hope, and love. Take another look at this well-known verse:

> "And so faith, hope, love abide [*faith*—conviction and belief respecting man's relation to God and divine things; *hope*—joyful and confident expectation of eternal salvation; *love*—true affection *for God* and *man, growing out of God's love for and in us*], these three; but

the greatest of these is love." (1 Corinthians 13:13, AMPC, emphasis added)

It's right there, as plain as day on the black and white of this page: "True affection for God and man, *growing out of God's love for and in us*"! Until we get a download of God's perfect, great, all-consuming love *for* **us**, we don't have what we need to truly love others. Once you get a revelation of **God loves me, yes, God loves me!**—then you contain His love **in** you. Only then can you start to truly love others. Only then can you really let people be people. It is then that you don't hold things over the people in our life, like: "You are too serious and need to lighten up, you're used to getting your way just like the baby you are, you're too this, you're too that," and so on.

So, how do you feel about your siblings? Has there been jealousy or fault-finding that needs to be dealt with so you can love them where they are? If you're an only child, do you need to examine your relationships to see if you're choosing people who will make you the center of attention—only to cause a raucous when things don't go your way? How about those "hard to get along with" people you have to be around? Are you pursuing the presence of God so you are filled up to overflowing with His love? After all, that's how we love the unlovely and the difficult ones in life. It's all about *God's love in us*. We cannot give away what we do not have.

Something I've learned and must be frequently reminded of is that people are not our enemies. At times, you may feel like the person you married is more of a foe than a friend. Difficult people and relationships could turn you bitter towards all people and hesitant to trust anyone. However, the enemy we fight is much different than the people we see and deal with in our lives. Ephesians 6:12 puts it this way:

"For our struggle is not against flesh and blood, but against the rulers, against the authorities, against the powers of this dark world and against spiritual forces of evil in the heavenly realms." (NIV)

We are warned to stand firm against that terrible adversary of ours. The devil is prowling around like a lion, waiting to get his foot in the door with our compromise, fence-straddling, and sin-dabbling. There are times he most definitely works through people to get to us. (Consider the weakest links in your spiritual garrison; be sure to surround yourself with sold-out, God-fearing believers who can battle in the right way with and for you—not against you.) The enemy's aim is to deceive us, divide us, devour us, and destroy us. In 1 Peter 5:9-10, we are cautioned and encouraged by this:

> "Stand *firm* against him, and be *strong* in your faith. Remember that your Christian brothers and sisters all over the world are *going through* the same kind of suffering you are. In His kindness God called you to share in

His eternal glory *by means of Christ Jesus.* So after you have suffered a *little* while, *He will* restore, support, and strengthen you, and *He will* place you on a firm foundation." (NLT, emphasis added)

My Brother, My Sister

When KB was a baby, I was terrified at the thought of having another baby. Things were still so rocky between Kelly and me then; I did not want to be alone taking care of two babies in diapers. As God restored our lives and our marriage, things got much better and we learned to take the "D" word out of our vocabulary: don't consider or threaten divorce. KB was such a good, easy baby. When asked about having another child, I would nervously say, "I don't know...," and joke around that another one could not be as easy as our baby girl. When she was around four years old, I began to desire having another child. We talked and prayed about it, and in March of 2011, I had another positive pregnancy test. We were ecstatic. We told family and everyone at church. About a week went by, and I began to bleed and miscarry.

I had figured the due date already, and it would have been 11-10-11. I had a t-shirt for KB that said "I'm the big sister," and we took a picture of her to send to family when we first told them. Looking back, I still remember the comfort and peace I felt during those painful, sad times. I told myself the things we try to rationalize: I wasn't very far along...the pregnancy tests didn't have very dark positive marks from the beginning...something just wasn't right. *Despite logic, heartache still hurts.* Love stepped up for me in those days of mourning and solitude. Love stepped up in my husband, who let me stay at home to rest while he went to church and work and into the community. He answered all the "Congratulations!" with what we now had to tell people. He cared for our little KB and ran the business and took care of household things, and he just let me be.

Love stepped up in my life during those days, as God comforted my heart and gave me a peace I still cannot put into words. I had some physical pain, yet was able to stay at home instead of going to the hospital or doctor's office. God took care of me in ways I didn't even know I needed. I sat in the recliner and watched a dozen episodes I had recorded of my favorite Bible teacher, Joyce Meyer. They were all timely messages I needed and was ready to receive. I had my favorite Bible beside me, and looked up things often that weekend as my body was going through the miscarriage. That's the Bible I still carry today. It's the New Living Translation Slimline I purchased right after I was born again. God has spoken to me so many times on this journey through His written Word.

*Here is a word of encouragement for you, my daughter, sister, or friend. If you're tired of defeat or have deep wounds—and you're *ready* for healing and renewal—the Word of God must have high priority in your life. As seasons come and go, sometimes you will spend more or less time reading the Bible. There will always be things vying for your time and attention. If you consistently learn to make God's Word your daily bread, you won't wake up one day almost spiritually starved to death. Think of it as your Bread of Life, and amazing insight to your friend, Jesus.*

KB was young, but understood that her brother or sister went on to Heaven because the baby couldn't stay here with us for some reason. Only God knows. My faith has grown over the years as I trust Him; I remind myself often that I'm not supposed to know and figure everything out. It is only God Who knows the whole scope of things from the beginning to the end. One thing trials do is help you have compassion for others going through similar things. I remember what it's like, not knowing if the symptoms every month are pregnancy related or premenstrual. I can't count all the months I didn't know if I should buy another pregnancy test or tampons, so I went through the checkout with both. Month after month, no test was needed. Each month I learned to trust God more and more.

In learning to deal with what I wanted and yearned for—another pregnancy and healthy baby, a sibling for KB, for our family to be fruitful and multiply—but didn't see come to pass, I simply had to say very often, "God, I trust You." Months have turned into years, and I've been trusting God with His plan for my life, while pursuing the passion He has put inside me. In ways, I'm like an expectant mother because

I know something is growing inside me. It is *hope*, and it's an eager expectation that *something good* is going to happen—today, and in my life, and into eternity.

We must take care of ourselves as women should when they have something wonderful growing on the inside. We can learn to be very cautious about what goes in our eyes, ears, and mouth. This isn't only for the things God is growing in us, but because young ears and eyes are taking in all we say and do. When KB says something I've said or mimics something I do, it's a reminder that our little miracle child is learning how to be a woman, a friend, a wife, and even a sister by watching me.

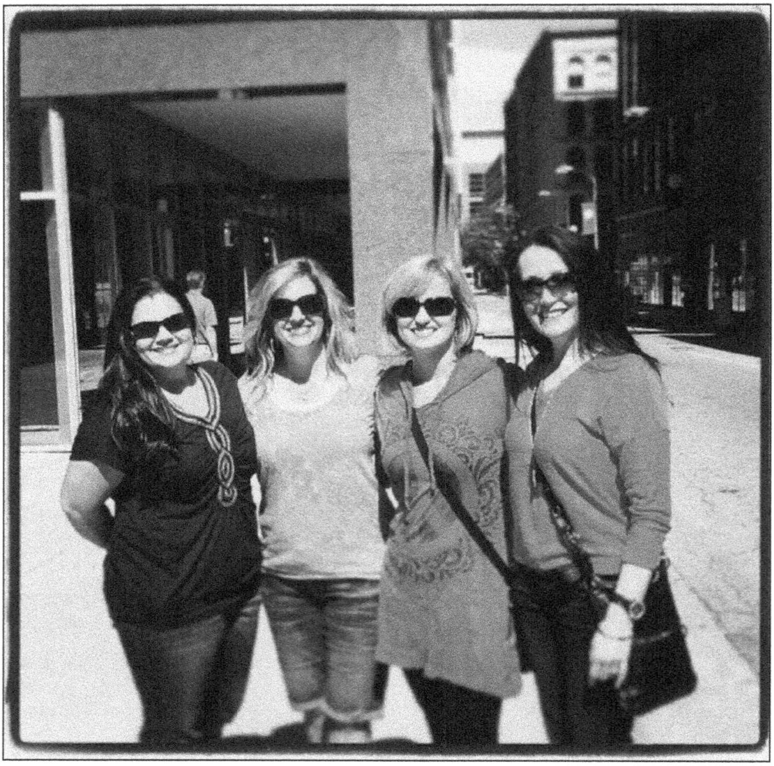

Chapter Five
Learning from My Sisters

I have grown to love, appreciate, and embrace having a larger family. Ours was just my sister and me, and we have always been pretty close (especially after she graduated college and we were on the same playing field). My mom and dad each came from homes with five children. We grew up being close to many of our aunts, uncles, and cousins. My family then grew even more with Kelly Shane and his brother and two sisters, their spouses, and nieces and nephews. Our family sized get-togethers are wonderful, no matter how many of us there are. When it is just the three of us—Kelly, KB, and me—I love that sweet, special family time of just us. When it's the holidays, I'm so thankful for the rooms full of family and the bond we have from spending life together. We always remember the ones who aren't with us, for whatever reason that may be. Some have other family to visit, and some have gone on to be with the Lord. Each one is so unique and touches all the rest of us in very special ways.

There's an extraordinary beauty God has created in us females. The sweet ladies in my life have taught me so much. My grandmother, Mamaw Keller, will be 96 on her next birthday. She is really sharp and remembers the names of all her grandchildren, great-grandchildren, and great-great-grandchildren. Mamaw Keller and I have always had a special connection; for years, I imagined Mamaw was staying the same and I was growing older. I just knew one day I would catch up with her and we would be two sweet little "ole" ladies going around, eating at our favorite restaurants, getting our Wal-Mart things, and laughing together. Age has been kind to her, and her attitude is phenomenal.

Several years ago, when she was still driving, she stopped at a fast food place for lunch. Someone asked her, "How old are you?" She told him, "If I sat around and thought about that, I might never get out of the house!" End of conversation. (He should have known better than to ask a lady her age, anyway. Way to go, Mamaw!) She dresses, does her hair and make-up, and puts on jewelry every day. She does her morning chores, and gets out on Saturdays for shopping and Sundays for Sunday School. Aunt Caroline is her chauffeur, and they get out together weekly as long as the weather is good. What a wonderful legacy this sweet lady has brought into our family!

My sweet, kind, patient, mother—who has been a nurse for decades—has a heart of gold and a spirit for adventure. She and my Kelly are a lot alike. Mama always reads the paper or hears about activities, festivals, trips—you name it—and is ready to go on the next pursuit. Between Kelly and Mama, I've finally gotten where I like to travel and see where the next quest will take us. Most recently, Mama has been joining me (or a group of us) in St. Louis, MO, for the Love Life Women's Conference. We look forward to that every year. We watch God at work in all the details of a trip like that; it's never short of amazing. There's something wonderful about getting away for a little while with lots of laughs and much-needed girl time.

My other mother, Brenda, is most likely the reason my husband has the heart he does. He got it from his Mom. When you see them, you are looking generosity and true concern in the face. Brenda is a phenomenal cook, and Kelly gets that from his mom, too. Brenda and Scotty did a great job raising their children. They taught their four kids about hard work and taking care of what you have. One of the greatest things about these wonderful people is their loyalty. They value friends and family, and no one feels like an outsider around them. *They have come to see all four of their kids experience the salvation of Jesus Christ.* The highlight of our time together is joining hands in a big circle and thanking God for Who He is, how He blesses us, and for our salvation.

The list goes on. Of course, Baby Sister is totally the best sister ever. Growing up together gave us such a special bond. Sometimes you just need to be around those people in life who "get it." I was blessed with other sisters when I married

Kelly. Monnie is an inspiration and fantastic educator; that woman has so much love to eagerly give. She raised two great, successful sons, which speaks volumes in itself. Now, my Cher; I love that woman. She adores KB like she is her own. (I've told her that when KB is older and it's not cool to talk to your mom about some things, as her Aunt Cher she can give good advice and make sure she is on the right path.) Cher and I made a pact one Sunday after church while eating at the Pickwick Landing State Park: we will be spiritual accountability partners.

Debbie is married to Andy, Kelly's brother. Deb is always so thoughtful to remember her sisters' birthdays, and gives the most special "happies," like jewelry, lotion, scarves, and stationery. Deb took such good care of Andy while he was in the hospital having most of his esophagus removed due to esophageal cancer. While writing and editing this book, Andy went on to be with the Lord. We found out on a Monday how rapidly and completely the cancer had spread; he took his last breath the following Saturday morning. You see love in action when families go through life together and draw closer during things like that. You also remember what is truly most important in life.

There's also a special group I call my Corinth Girls. Christie, Gidget, Amy, Leigh Ann, Coco and I were big trouble back in the day. Our friendship has survived the storms of divorce, moving, busyness, and family life in general. We try to get together once or twice a year, but sometimes a letter sent or Christmas card mailed is the extent of it. No matter the time that passes, we can catch up on things in a couple of hours when we do get together. They are the kind of friends you want to be there for, and you know they will be there for you, too.

We can learn from and share life with many lovely ladies. Just think of those who our faithful Father has put in your life—for a season, or for the long haul. You may have a Cherrie, who is up for coffee any time and simply makes you smile. You may have a Tammy, who is good at the hard things where you work and helps you to manage money better. You may have a Verna, who teaches you the Word of God from a humble heart; when you see her and embrace, you instantly think about how good Heaven will be and your heart is thankful.

You may have a Mamaw Bryant, who died when you were young. She still impacts you with early memories of sleepovers, playing outside until dark, and her wonderful cooking. You may have a Geri, who represents family torn apart by the enemy. She is now miraculously reconciled to you as a dear sister in Christ. You may have a Nickie, Haley, or Molly in their early years of adulthood. These are the young ladies who need to see *lived out* what it means to be a wife, mother, friend, and sister...how to be a woman, and most importantly, a woman of God.

With some, you are acquaintances. With others, you have deep connections. God has placed many beautiful women in our lives. There is a generation of girls who need to learn from us—from our triumphs *and* our mistakes. They can learn from our transparency. They can see how a wife is to love her husband. They can see love at work through the imperfections. Even though they will have to learn many of the tough lessons on their own, it's a powerful thing to let them know *they are not alone* in it. We all go through things, and *we are stronger together*.

For the Love of My Sisters

When Kaleigh Brooke was a baby and toddler, I was able to stay home with her for the most part. We own a seasonal boating business, and family usually watched her on summer weekends and holidays so I could help my husband at work. A few months before KB turned three years old, she started preschool. She went on Mondays, Wednesdays, and Fridays until she was five years old. In those early days of being a mother, I really poured my heart out to God about wanting Kelly to step up and be the man I knew he could be. I quickly realized (but slowly admitted) that I was the one who needed to change.

It was like some "Dr. Phil meets Oprah" conversation in my mind: you can't change somebody else, you can only change *you*. By that point in our marriage, I had gotten fed up with the mess in my mind and our marriage. After a terrible fight with Kelly—one of those yelling matches where nobody wins but everyone is wounded—I was desperate for change.

Not knowing where to begin, my thoughts led to this: "My Mama had *us* in church; I need to get that baby in church!"

I remember being at the kitchen sink when it hit me. ***You need to get that baby in church!*** It must have been a direct message from God downloaded to my heart, because I knew nothing at that time about hearing from God or being led by the Holy Spirit.

There was an intense inner battle before we attended church together the first time. Growing up as a Methodist gave me comfort, traditions, and expectations I didn't want to let go of, even at the price of getting our daughter in church. My goodness! The gut-wrenching feeling of giving in to Kelly and going to a Baptist church (like he attended some while growing up) made my stubbornness flare up and out. I went for the love of our child, and eventually we joined there. Inside, I was fighting it tooth and nail. Lots of times those first visits I wouldn't let Kelly open the door for me, because my attitude was: "You never help or do anything kind for me at home, so don't think you're gonna do it for people to see, buster!" That's the attitude I carried around for months and years (and it was constant and even worse in my mind).

It was in that safe place of a caring church body I began to hear the Word of God and feel convicted like never before. Inspired by God's Word, that Phil-Oprah phrase became: you can't change somebody else, *and you can't even change yourself **without the power of God at work in your life**.* It's in that particular church building—as people came together to sing about God, hear great messages, pray, and fellowship—I learned about having many brothers and sisters in Christ. Attending church is a great place to start. (It's so important to be around other believers; we are made for community.) It opened the truth of God's Word to me as I sat under anointed teaching and preaching. God used church attendance, along with listening to some of my favorite teachers and preachers on TV and podcasts, to give me a longing to hear His Word, and be convicted when necessary. And, oh, was I ever convicted!

You must understand that conviction is not condemnation, because Romans 8:1 says, "So now there is no condemnation for those who belong to Christ Jesus." (NLT) If you are burdened by guilt and shame, the last things you need are guilt-trips and shame-based behavior modification. You need to hear the truth of God's Word, and how to stop living in your cycle of sin and shame. The word seems so simple, but should be heavily considered: *repent*! Once you step out, away from the sin that is pulling you down and destroying your life, you go in the *opposite* direction. Then, the next one is a four-letter word you must learn to embrace: *obey*. (I will go into some more detail about this journey of repentance and obeying in the next chapter. Here's a sneak peak: God is so amazing!)

As I was learning and soaking up the Word, some very dear sisters came into my life. They have poured their wisdom and knowledge into me and others. Being around them perks my spirit up, because we are on this earthly mission field together—going through life's pain and joys together. God was speaking to me through His Word and the still, small voice I was longing to hear. I wanted to do something big for God, and once again He so sweetly put this on my heart as I was walking into the bathroom at home. *Use this time to keep on learning and studying as much of the Word as you can.* I knew this was straight from the Lord. I can still picture where I was, leaning over a drawer to put something up. God whispered to my heart, and I held on to what He said for those years our daughter was in preschool.

There was such contentment in life when I heard and obeyed God. (It's been years, and I *still* know this to be true.) I wasn't content to the point of not wanting to change. However, there was peace in *knowing* I was right with God. It was up to Him to do the transformation in me; my part was to press in to Him, abide in Him, and press on in life. This is not something that good works or being "good enough" can get you; there's no real contentment found there. This is about accepting the Way—through Jesus—that God has made for you, then trusting Him to help you walk in it.

Finally, I was learning to walk in the peace and joy that only come from the love of Jesus. I began to study more, in addition to listening to others teach. I went to as many Bible studies as my schedule allowed. Since most of the toxicity in my head eventually slipped out of my mouth, God began this transformation deep on the inside. He led me to Scripture to replace the negative chatter in my mind. During this, I began to realize the astounding importance of our thought life. It's such a battle to take those thoughts captive and make sure they line up with the Word of God; *it is so worth the fight*! It was life changing to realize I didn't have to think whatever fell in my head. I could change my thoughts and the atmosphere around me if I learned to think on *and say* God's Word, and not dwell on my thoughts, feelings, and emotions.

To find answers, I broke down the areas of my day looking for reasons I stayed defeated. I spent mornings getting ready and thought about negative things the entire time. This area of defeat dwelled on how I had been mistreated, what my husband "wasn't" or didn't do, what someone said to me, what I should have said back, etc. My day was ruined before I left the house! I went out with a pessimistic, defensive attitude. Another area was from being habitually late. In the car, I was always *mentally rehearsing* why I was late and the excuses for it. I seemed to have no concept of building margin into my day, or controlling what I thought. It was all very exhausting. Conviction set in that I was full of pride and completely selfish. (Pride always leads to demise. Selfish people will not be happy.) So my study began there, at the root of these problems: my thoughts. One of the first verses I learned to battle those negative, nagging thoughts, I still use today:

> "Don't copy the behavior and customs of this world, but *let God transform you* into a new person *by changing the way you think*. Then you will learn to know God's will for

you, which is good and pleasing and perfect."
(Romans 12:2, NLT, emphasis added)

The day came that our daughter would start kindergarten. I had been training her up, learning to be a maker and maintainer of peace in our home, and I knew I would not cry—but rejoice—that she would be in school five days a week. Don't get me wrong. I loved staying home with her those years. It was often so challenging when I felt unappreciated by my husband, and "less than" because I was not at the office like him. Those days were invaluable because I was able to pour into our daughter like no one else could. As the Lord was teaching me to step it up—as a woman of God, a wife, a mother, a daughter, and a sister—our sweet daughter was a direct recipient of my growth. She was also the one I apologized to most often from the times I was frustrated, frazzled, and she saw me blow up. If you're a mom, you understand this completely.

About a week before school started, a dear sister in Christ called me. Linda asked if I would be interested in going a few miles down the road into Iuka, MS, to a place called Pray Pottery. She, Suzanne, and I could share our testimonies and teach during the lunch hour on Thursdays for the month of August. I was so elated that God opened the door at that time! I had been doing what He said last: *Use this time to keep on learning and studying as much of the Word as you can.*

I did just that for a few years with a small child at home. Now, He was giving me an opportunity to come under some seasoned, godly women who had loved the Lord for many years. He was giving me the grace and ability to share the powerful testimony as a person once trapped in darkness, who is now living fully in God's beautiful light. You know what else? That one month has turned into five years of continual Thursdays at Pray Pottery. I'm thankful to Rhonda and Lauren for loving God and being obedient to His good and perfect plans for them and Pray Pottery. I'm so thankful for women coming together to praise God for Who He is, and to learn together, laugh together, cry together, and pray together. I am so very thankful for the many sisters He has put in our lives. This God of ours, oh my, He is just so good!

the CO

THURSDAY ■ APRIL 16, 2015

Inves

Ron Schaming
Managing Editor
schaming@courier

Savannah resi
land is facing a
murder after al

Main Stre

Inspirational
With the National Day of Prayer being celebrated in three weeks, on May 7, Kim Edge has been especially grateful for how prayer has changed her life.

—Read More, 1B

Chapter Six

The Prodigal and the Parent

It happened in a moment; as I walked through the kitchen, the stupor lifted. It settled on me for five months after Kaleigh Brooke was born, then immediately lifted. Some call it postpartum depression. It was like going through the motions in a clouded haze. I was in a funk. Whatever it was, it was thick and consuming. Like the dark depression I went through in my teens and twenties, that feeling of depression was tangible and overwhelming. My mind was in a fog, but something in me must have had hope—a hope it wouldn't last forever. It really felt like those days would last without end: 2 a.m. feedings, a suitcase-sized diaper bag for the simplest outing, taking sporadic showers while watching the baby monitor the entire time.

I bought a small digital camera and began taking pictures of all the cuteness of a baby girl. There were photos of her sleeping on her boppy, sleeping on the bed with pillows all around, going for a boat ride, buckled in her car seat, adventures we embarked on with Grandmama, just lots and lots of pictures. I printed and put them in several photo albums, looking forward to a day I could look back and remember—without the numb fog enveloping me. That day came, although everything in me felt like it never would.

On one of KB's baby visits, the doctor prescribed an antidepressant for me. I stuck the prescription in a drawer, planning to fill it at a later date. I'm not sure why I didn't jump at the chance to get a pill to help me; probably the main reason is because I was breastfeeding. I also believe my head began to clear up during pregnancy from all the substances I had previously taken, both prescription and illegal. Then, WHAM! Your body doesn't know what's about to hit during those months of growing a new life inside.

A woman's hormones are a peculiar thing. They leave you hysterically giddy, crying your eyes out, a hot mess, or somewhere in between. I never got back on medication, which was a miracle considering my history. I'm so thankful my mind had a chance to heal and learn the right way to think and meditate. There are cases where people need the help. I believe there is a time and situation for that. Ultimately, we must remember that no pill can give us peace—peace of heart and mind—like our God can give.

On this journey, we can learn to seek God and His counsel for what is best. If we're seeking and following His will, *He* will *guide* us to the right answers. Sometimes it is through the medical technology God has given us. Sometimes it's a matter of spiritual wholeness and well-being. The thing about recovery is *you need it, but you don't have to stay there.* Get help when needed. Learn to go to our great Helper first, because He knows you like no one else. Make up your mind to recover from life's hardships, and don't stay a victim. Then, make it a point to *help someone else while you're healing.* So many times in life, we are unable to help ourselves. Our help truly does come from the Lord, and from those people He works through to help and encourage us. This is a spiritual truth God will show you time and time again, if you allow Him.

What Is Your Answer?

"Today I have given you the choice between life and death, between blessings and curses. Now I call on heaven and earth to witness the choice you make. Oh, that you would choose life, so that you and your descendants might live! You can make this choice by loving the LORD your God, obeying him, and committing yourself firmly to him. This is the key to your life. And if you love and obey the LORD, you will live long in the land the LORD swore to give your ancestors Abraham, Isaac, and Jacob." (Deuteronomy 30:19-20, NLT)

We must each make the decision for whom we are living. Not choosing is just the choice to reject His Life. I've mentioned the battles raging within me because of rebellion, pride, and taking offense whenever the opportunity arose. Sadly, being offended can happen anytime with anyone in any situation. This eats away at sound thinking because you're led astray with emotions and how you feel. I was the queen of emotional chaos. So many times I'd find things in this world to feed the chaos.

I relate to people listening to what stirs their soul. (I took pride in being a teen "head banger" because I listened to the melodious, dark undertones and lyrics of death metal, like Metallica and Megadeth.) Eventually, I came to see how worldly music—even if it's just the good beat or twangy sound you like—can cloud your decisions and desensitize your soul. I've discovered so many uplifting Christian artists with any sound you like; there's no need to go back to music that will drag you down. We are bombarded from within and from without, and too often we don't know *how* to guard our heart from the big and small things trying to steal it away.

You do realize this is a battle for your soul, right? If our adversary can keep you deceived, arrogant, in a defeated mindset, in a monotonous routine, or a numb state of mind, he will do just that. He doesn't have to make you so evil you obviously know you're on a slippery slope between Heaven and Hell. In his book *The Screwtape Letters*, C. S. Lewis wrote, "Indeed the safest road to Hell is the gradual one—the gentle slope, soft underfoot, without sudden turnings, without milestones, without signposts..."[1] When you are confronted by a holy God, a decision must be made.

When the fear of staying the same became greater than the fear of change, something was jarred inside me. For my personality, there was comfort in routine. Change was not a pleasant word at all. Have you ever found yourself in a dreadful cycle of things being okay for a while, then <u>always</u> going back to problems that are never dealt with and confronted in the right way? The battle could be for your soul, or for your peace and joy. I have felt ripped apart from the desperate need to have it all—my soul, joy, and peace—secure in the hands of our Almighty God.

When we started going to church, even with my bad attitude and reluctance to trust, I had the desire to change. God gave me a heart that began to tenderize at His Word. Keep in mind, I got offended *a lot* at the Word and things I heard preached. One example is when the message included Scripture about baptism, like when John baptized Jesus. I was highly offended, and thought: "That's just like those Baptists to go there and preach that."

Here is the amazing part God did through the truth of His Word. I got home and began to read it for myself! My argument was that I was sprinkled as a baby and confirmed at 12 with a whole group of my peers. My feathers were so ruffled, even though I had just been baptized in order to join the church we were attending. It was my heart attitude that was all wrong. In reading and studying for myself, God began to soften and tenderize my heart of stone and callousness. The Truth of His Word was unfolding in my brokenness and my seeking. A decision was imminent.

After hearing good, sound preaching straight from the Word of God and inspired by the Holy Spirit, I found myself at another crossroads. This time, the very core of my beliefs was being tested. Here's the verse that stung and begged for more thought and answers: "Jesus said to him, I am the **Way** and the **Truth** and the **Life**; no one comes to the Father except by (through) Me." (John 14:6, AMPC)

A little background will shed some light on my search for Truth...

While teaching at Corinth Jr. High and High School in my early to mid-twenties, I decided to get my Master of Education degree. During those couple of years at a Christian university, I had challenged the written Bible studies that were part of the curriculum with my own notes penciled in to the side. I had even met with a Dean of Education concerning how a good God could let a good person go to Hell, just because she was a different denomination. (I didn't even know to bring Jesus up in the conversation; I was blinded by religion.) I won't go into the lengths of it, but he expressed how that idea somewhat varied among different congregations of their denomination. I still had not gotten to the heart of the matter after all those years.

Fast forward a decade, and the words of the Bible stood strong without wavering. Forget arguing about the good moral traits of any person on this planet. This was not about us ever being good enough. I had a choice to make: would I take this Scripture for what it said, or twist it to reflect what I wanted it to say? I had reached the heart of the matter: Jesus is the only Way to the Father; it is only He Who brings salvation to our souls. What I once even claimed was close-mindedness now shone in the Light as TRUTH.

Sitting in church one Sunday morning—early in my search for the Lord—I chose to believe what the Word of God says over what I can explain or what I think and feel. I could not live double-minded anymore, picking the parts I liked and ignoring or disregarding the parts that offended me or didn't make sense yet. That was another huge step in my journey, even on a seemingly ordinary Sunday. Yet, that was the day—the moment—I decided to believe what the Word of God says. I believe the Holy Bible is God's inerrant Word to us, without flaw, and I bank my entire life, future, and hope on it. God increased my faith that day. Doubt was out the door. It was monumental.

Week after week and month after month, I took our baby to church. I would invite Kelly, but many times he stayed out most of the night before drinking or partying with good ole boys from the area. Often, I would give him the option to go with us, knowing it was like a stab in the chest because he openly and obviously wasn't doing right—and we both knew it. After months of going to church the desire only got stronger for God to *change me*. I quit asking Kelly to go to church with us, but he knew we were going. I quit playing his conscience to do this or do that (or stop doing this or that). He recalls that time in a different way, from a guy's perspective; it was "the week I stopped nagging him." Call it what you want, but it was God at work. I was learning to trust God to change me, and finally realized if Kelly were to ever change, it would *have* to be God's doing. I turned my husband over to God, and prayed for him like never before.

I'd like to say things got better and easier for us soon after that, but I want you to understand something. Many times when God is dealing with someone, things get worse before they get better. You may pray for someone and—according to their actions—think there's no hope for change. God does not give us the privilege to stop praying for someone. However, you may have to distance yourself if there is physical danger involved, or someone tears you apart verbally and emotionally. Abuse is never acceptable.

What's On Your Mind?

Thinking back to how awful and scary the year of 2008 was—then the amazing work God did in our lives, and how He began to restore our marriage—I wrote a post on Facebook. Here's how it went:

January 30, 2012

[Status = What's on your mind?] The story of how grapes saved my marriage:

[Comments:] ...well, if that got your attention, you should hear that it was God Who saved my marriage. But here's how it started...

In a last-ditch effort about 4 years ago, I "tricked" Kelly into going on the Counce FBC marriage retreat where there would be quail hunting, fishing, horseback riding, etc. The 'et cetera' were Steve and Debbie Wilson (Marriage Matters Now founders) who were going to be at a quaint little resort area on the lake in Alabama.

Before there was a chance to do any of the extracurricular activities, I broke down sobbing and let all my fears, doubts, and disappointments out. Blah! There you have it, husband. Of course, he responded with some anger, self-defense, and disappointments himself. It was a start. Then in one large group session, Steve said something that would change us forever. As he pointed up and to himself, up and to himself, he said, "Until you get things right this way, you can't get things right this way..." and pointed back and forth to Debbie and himself.

It made such a huge impact on Kelly; he often shares that story today. Another life-changing thing we did at the marriage retreat was *pray* in each other's ear. It was Kelly's turn to sob this time. That weekend brought healing and truth to each of us. We realized we weren't alone at all in the struggles that men and women face. It brought unity and life into a sorrowful, dying marriage. It was important to get away from the responsibilities of everyday life and all the demands that are brought on us daily.

This was when I realized how much I needed to change, also. Maybe I no longer shared in the drugs and boozing it up, but my thought life was so toxic. Also, I placed total responsibility on Kelly for making me happy. On top of that, I had high, unrealistic expectations that were raised higher and higher each time he "failed." Little did I realize, he was set up to feel like a failure over and over. Eventually, he gave up trying to please me.

As we each began our journey of seeking God and happiness through Him, we treated each other kinder, more tenderly, and our home became a place of comfort, stability, and fun. We realize this is not a one-time thing of doing right, being kind, and minimally getting by. *When you decide giving up is not an option*, God will give you the grace and strength you need to continue in hard times or a difficult relationship. Being a true Christian doesn't make it easier, but it gives you the chance that you wouldn't have if you do it the world's way.

Today, I'm smiling about the grapes. They represent the little things in life. When Kelly got his heart right with Jesus, he slowly started changing from the inside out. On his journey to lose weight and feel better and healthier, he ate lots of fruit, meat, and water...no sugar, carbs, or bread. It resulted in a 70 lb. weight loss. Grapes are something he likes washed, pulled off the stem, and put in a gallon Ziploc bag in the refrigerator.

He's been hunting a lot in Arkansas this month. When he got home last night, I made sure there was a full, gallon bag of grapes ready for him.

You see, it's not the grapes. It's that I don't sit around stewing over what I don't have or what others aren't doing for me. It's about, "What can I do for someone else?" In 1 Corinthians 10:24, Paul says, "Don't be concerned for your own good but for the good of others." Then in Romans 12:21, we have the key to our strategy: "Don't let evil conquer you, but conquer evil by doing good." (NLT)

I may be in the right, while someone else does something obviously wrong; that's no excuse for me to behave wrong with *my* attitude, words, or actions. A lot of prayer went into our marriage as it was falling apart. It was my last resort. Now prayer goes into every aspect as I know and learn how to pray for my husband, our child, family, and friends. You can turn your marriage around or make any relationship better by being who YOU are called to be *in Christ*. Through the thick and thin of it, God will be your Source. May you use some "grapes" and other good fruit to turn your life into a sweeter place for yourself and those around you!

Is There Still Time?

If you have people in your life who seem hopelessly bound by alcohol, drugs, depression, or worldliness, there is still hope. Do you know why? They are still breathing.

Even as I was on a ventilator over a dozen years ago, there was hope for me. I had not gotten desperate enough in the search, nor allowed myself to be clearheaded enough to hear the life-saving message of Jesus Christ and believe. Hope was still there. Hope has no other choice but to remain. First Corinthians 13:13 says, "And now these three remain: faith, hope and love. But the greatest of these is love." (NIV)

You may be the parent, exhausted in body, mind, and resources. Please know that our heavenly Father knows your heart. He knows if you feel the blame for someone's bad choices. He knows if you're at your wits' end. He is a kind, merciful God, and He wants the best for you and those you love. Our finite minds can scarcely take in the astounding love and goodness God has made available to us. Please rest assured, dear friend, that *He is at work*. Let Him be at work in and through you. Do all the crisis demands, then stand firm on the promises of God. Only He can make a way when there seems no way. Lean on your good Father. Rely on Him as your Source. Throw your burdens and cares at the foot of His cross. When you are weary, rest in Him. He is faithful to keep you and sustain you. He will guard you and guide you.

You may be the one who thought the grass was greener on the other side. Come to find out, you have to mow there, too. There's probably a lot more fertilizing manure than you expected. Our merciful, heavenly Father is waiting with open arms for the worst, strung out addict, and the "well thought of" person who doesn't want to admit his or her need for Him.

Jesus came to be the Savior for each of us. The devil has his schemes; sadly, we are naïve to many of these. However, human nature—by its own free will—severs us from abundant life with God now...and into eternity.

Romans 8:38-39 says, "For I am convinced that neither death nor life, neither angels nor demons, neither the present nor the future, nor any powers, neither height nor depth, nor anything else in all creation, will be able to separate us from the love of God that is in Christ Jesus our Lord." (NIV) *God's love is here!* It is readily available for you, and can work *in* and *through* you. The choice is yours. You have the very breath of God in you, my friend. Please make it count!

Born Again

I want to share something that few people know. I played the role of good wife and mother for a while without truly having my heart right with God. In the "grapes" story, I may have come across like Kelly mainly had the huge mess to see and fix. My mess was a sneaky one, though, just hidden under the surface. I was like the multitude of "good people" you see all around. They seem to do pretty well in life on their own (and I mean: apart from God). They may even act religious about church attendance or be modest in their dress. They are the ones who'd give the shirts off their backs and seem to have things figured out. Be aware; they don't! I didn't! I had learned to look and act the part.

After Kelly full-heartedly surrendered to Jesus at the marriage conference, God was really working on me. I knew deep down inside I was baptized only to join the congregation. The Word had revealed Truth to me for months as I sought and devoured what I could take in. One morning, Kelly and a friend taught our Sunday School class. No one knew the battle within me. The drawing of the Lord to get my heart right was undeniable. I rationalized everything that morning:

- What would it look like *now* to go forward saying I need salvation after all this time in church?
- When I was 15 or 16, I heard a moving message with my friends at FBC's Revival in Corinth. Surely I believed then...
- When the pastor announces his retirement, that would be a sweet time to go up and ask him for prayer.

As I sat next to Kelly in the morning service on February 22, 2009, I could almost hear a little devil on one shoulder and an angel on the other. "You're ok! What would it look like now? You can wait." Then, sweetly, "Do you want to go on like this? Stand up. Take the first step." My face had flashes of surging heat and my heart pounded in my chest. As soon as the preacher ended his sermon, I jumped up to make sure "I knew that I knew that I knew" I was saved. To my surprise, Kelly jumped up too and we just about ran down the aisle together. Maybe I floated. (Or that may have been over the next few days.) As I prayed out loud, chains fell off. They weren't visible in the physical realm, but I remember having the thought for a long time afterward: "I feel like a ton of bricks has been lifted off of me…"

Not that it matters about the order, but Kelly was born again first. After getting his heart right with God at the marriage retreat, he knew he had been baptized for the wrong reasons and now wanted to make it right. Little did I know then, but he almost didn't wait until the end of the service. He contemplated going up as soon as the service started. He could barely wait to say he needed baptized, now that his heart was right with God. I was more reluctant and stubborn to openly admit my need for a Savior—that I didn't have it all figured out. There was never a time I had accepted the love of God. Therefore, there was never any lasting fruit of a soul saved by Jesus. Salvation always brings about change.

Since the day I believed and openly declared that Jesus is Lord, there has always been a next step to take. The Holy Spirit so sweetly and tenderly puts things on your heart, just when He knows you're ready. It's as if He whispers, "It's time." It does need to be mentioned here that just because God is gently guiding you, it doesn't mean you will feel a gentleness in your soul. There will be major conflict inside. Your mind, will, and emotions don't want to be harnessed or care that you're a new creation in Christ. They just know it's painful and uncomfortable. The old ways and habits will fight to the death.

For me, the next step was baptism. I was reading the Bible, learning to pray some, and just knew. On April 12, 2009, my sweetheart and I were baptized in Pickwick Lake. Had I not said yes to God, it scares me to think where I'd be today. Since then, God has gently been guiding and showing me the next step. Thank God, in His mercy and patience, He called my name and allowed me to answer: "Yes, Lord!" May my answer always be, "Yes, Lord!"

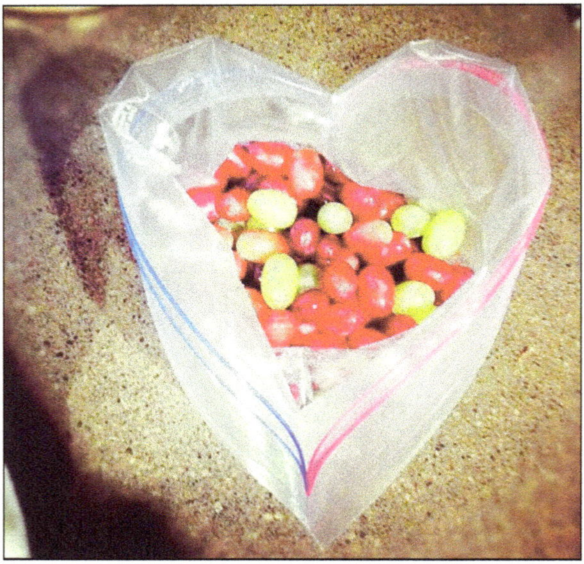

Chapter Seven

Good Fruit

For someone who only knew the addict side of my life, you could not explain writing a book called *Something Wonderful*. When I first began sharing my testimony, there was a shock factor that I could really have been that bad and that depressed. Even in this book, I couldn't go into detail about how bad it really was. That's partly because I can't find the words, and partly because I don't want to relive all of that darkness. I'm careful not to hash out all those details very often. However, it is good to remember how far God has brought us. When you've been pulled from the pit, it makes the praise even sweeter!

There was freedom and power in facing the truth about me. God opened doors and equipped me to share with careful vulnerability. By careful, I mean that there was a season I told many details about my alcohol abuse and drug addiction. After some time, those details left a bad taste in my mouth. On the inside, God was working in me and growing me to a point where I could share openly, but without all the details. Sharing my testimony became 10% of the way *I was*, plain and simple: it was sin. As my faith and love grew, 90% focused on *how great God is*.

If you ever start to take a "pity trip" or "poor me vacation," spend time on purpose thinking about where God has brought you from, and how you've grown in the process. I heard someone say being self-focused all the time is just a form of idolatry. I didn't know if I should agree or be offended. Over time, I tend to agree with that because a selfish, self-centered person is not consumed with the things of God, but of self. Oh man, how I lived that firsthand for years! All that time of depression and concern for my feelings and my emotions did nothing for the glory of our God. Instead, I stayed in a prison cell that Jesus had already declared open. I just didn't have the eyes to see it then.

Something Strange

> "Dear friends, don't be surprised at the fiery trials you are going through, as if something strange were happening to you. Instead, be very glad—for these trials make you partners with Christ in his suffering, so that you will have the wonderful joy of seeing his glory when it is revealed to all the world. If you are insulted because you bear the name of

Christ, you will be blessed, for the glorious Spirit of God rests upon you. If you suffer, however, it must not be for murder, stealing, making trouble, or prying into other people's affairs. But it is no shame to suffer for being a Christian. Praise God for the privilege of being called by his name!" (1 Peter 4:12-16, NLT)

Did you read that?! Let's go back and read it again, slowly...

Peter said volumes here. Most likely, God is speaking to your heart about something specific or a few things of great importance through those verses. Now is a good time to let you in on something. (You most likely know this if you've been walking in faith as a Christian for any length of time.) *This Life as a sold-out follower of Christ is not an easy one.* Though it's not easy, it is simple. And, it is worth it! Our souls have been purchased at the highest price: the blood of God's one and only Son...*Jesus*. We cannot even begin to realize the eternal value of an on-fire soul consumed *by* and *for* the things of God. We should be led by the Holy Spirit all along the Way, and He will bring us comfort and peace throughout the journey. As we seek God daily, choices are set before us. We simply choose to obey, or not.

Obedience comes with a certain standard; compromise is no longer acceptable. Those of us who ask Jesus to be our Savior and Lord understand repentance. We turn from our sinful ways. When we are born again—in that instant—we have the Seed of Christ living in us! With a heart of overflowing gratitude, a shift takes place. Now you want to please God because of *His great love for you* (and not to obey laws or some religious set of guidelines.) To gain revelation that **God loves you** is a kick-start for LOVE and all the good fruit now available in you *through Christ.*

In Galatians 5:22-23, we see all that is ours: "But the Holy Spirit produces this kind of fruit in our lives: love, joy, peace, patience, kindness, goodness, faithfulness, gentleness, and self-control. There is no law against these things!"(NLT) Before you ever say something like, "I just don't have any self-control" or "I have zero patience," think about your words. As a born-again believer, you have the Seed of everything that Christ is *in you*! Maybe what you really meant was, "I don't want to suffer some now for a better outcome later." Come on, now. It's the truth that sets you free. When you come to terms with how you're thinking and seeing yourself, you can get past the excuses.

Ouch! This hurts!

We could not get enough of the Word and going to church. Sunday mornings, Sunday nights, and Wednesday nights were not enough. Kelly has always had a generous heart. Put that with his ability to think outside the box and see the bigger picture, and it was only a matter of time before he was all-in helping people in our community. He has a heart to help other men and families who are ravaged by addiction and brokenness. We started going to a local community center on Tuesday nights. The ministry was wonderful for families or individuals to request prayer, share a meal together, hear testimonies, and attend one of several classes offered.

I should be ashamed to say this, but I was more hesitant in committing to serve with this ministry. Social settings were never my favorite; Kelly seemed to flourish in them. I had longed for a time that my man would step up and be the leader in our home, so I went against my discomfort and said *Yes*. I was saying Yes again to the Lord, and Yes to serve beside my husband. God was good at shaking me out of my comfort zone. I could have never guessed in a million years at the shaking that was to come...

Kelly and I took something else with us from the marriage retreat I had "tricked him" into attending. That was where we first experienced healing and restoration, but there was *more*. Another first for us was *having fun while being sober*. There was a bonfire and cooler of iced-down soft drinks and water. That still stands out in my mind after all these years. We had never seen people—normal people, from a church, not all religious acting—who were having fun, laughing, standing on a sandy beach on an Alabama lake...sober! I want to stress: no alcohol!

We wanted more! The next year, Kelly made all the arrangements to go to a marriage conference in Gainesville,

GA. He got the tickets, reserved a hotel room, made sure someone could watch our baby girl, boarded our sweet dogs, and drove us there in February—our anniversary month. Not only did we hunger and thirst for the righteousness of God, but we were learning to enjoy life together and have fun in the best way possible...in God's way!

During the week, we could not wait for church and ministry meetings. I was asked to teach some during the ladies' Bible study at the community center. Kelly had been invited to go to the Ramp in Hamilton, AL, a few times with a friend. He got so much from the marriage conferences that he decided to go to this youth conference. His world was wrecked—in a very good way—during those meetings. Kelly experienced the presence of God in a way that left him changed forever. He was filled with the Holy Spirit. I didn't understand what was going on at the time, but it was evident at home he was a changed man. A wife knows when it's for real, and time will tell. Kelly encountered people at the Ramp devoted to God and to prayer. They have a heart for this generation to know the freedom and life that is available and abundant in Jesus Christ. So much is trying to strip our young people of their time and identity, and Kelly could relate.

On the other hand, I was skeptical for a while. God was building something up in me that only came out as a whispered prayer. "More of You, God. I just want more of You, God." After going to the summer Forward Conference and some Ramp worship services with Kelly, God answered my heart's cry and filled me to overflowing with His Holy Spirit. *I've never been the same since.* I once could say I knew about God; now *I know Him.* The thought of Him and His presence has not been far away—even during the dry seasons—since I was baptized with the Holy Spirit. Even when I "don't feel it," I still seek Him. I live beyond my feelings and *trust Him.* He is forever faithful.

Some of the places we go to worship are considered *charismatic.* The Encarta Dictionary defines that as: seeking direct spiritual experiences.[2] Not only did we seek them, we expected them. We had experienced God's healing power in our own lives and marriage, and we knew there was always *more* with God. Kelly unexpectedly got an ultimatum one day: stop going to the Ramp and listening to any of their sermons, or step down from the ministry on Tuesdays and any teaching at the church. At the least, he was devastated. I've never seen my man so torn and gut-wrenched as he prayed and fasted for a whole week until he made his choice. It had to be his choice. (I watched, waited, and prayed.) He could not wrap his mind around never listening to messages that called him out and challenged him to be a real man of God. He didn't want to sneak listening to CD sermons that helped him grow in his relationship with God. My husband chose to please God and seek Him, and not the approval and acceptance of man.

That was a detrimental time for him. He could have thrown in the towel and said that's enough of church politics and church things. He pressed on, and loves the Lord so much. We still love to visit many congregations of fellow believers in Christ. Kelly often reminds me: "Eat the fish and spit out the bone." We must test everything with the Word to make sure it is Truth.

Eventually my time came, and I got a phone call with an ultimatum: quit going or quit teaching. As ridiculous as it sounded, the option was to stop going with my husband to worship and seek God at these places so I could continue to teach. I, too, chose to please God and seek Him, and not the approval of man. It hurt so deeply—rejection from fellow servants of Christ. As time has a way of dealing with our wounds, healing and restoration did come, even from those painful days.

I know without a doubt God grew me by leaps and bounds during that time of heartache and exclusion. The testing was painful; the trials were long. Over time, God healed our hearts and gave us His forgiveness to extend to others and to receive with grace. We learned to respect and honor authority. Please remember: unless you learn to come *under* authority, you're never fit to be *in* authority. It didn't happen overnight, but we have no bitterness; God has a way of working ALL THINGS together for our good and His glory. God restored and strengthened those relationships over time. It is a beautiful picture of God "growing us up" and uniting the Body of Christ. As strange as it may sound, Kelly and I both agree we would not change those past hurts because we grew so much and saw God work wonders among His people.

People will hurt you; *never* use that as an excuse not to serve God and seek His will for your life. You fall under the category of people, so you will hurt others, too. Along this journey, you'll need to give and receive mercy. You do this because God lives in you. It's not always easy, but it's worth it.

Count the number of times you see *love* in the following passage:

> "Beloved, let us *love* one another, for *love* is from God; and everyone who *loves* is born of God and knows God. The one who does not *love* does not know God, for God is *love*." (1 John 4:7-8, NASB)

We won't always understand the reasons and timing for closed doors. Our part is to trust God and walk through the open doors—not bang our heads against the closed ones.

Through the years, I've been thankful that I learned early on to seek God and worship Him in the Secret Place of my heart, not waiting for some conference or service to fulfill this desire. It is a wonderful blessing to worship our God with a few (or a few thousand) believers with the same heartbeat for Him. Stay connected to the Church, for these brothers and sisters are the Body of Christ at work on the planet today. We each have certain gifts, talents, and strengths that are valuable to the Kingdom of God.

The Lord sure has His ways to keep me out of my comfort zone and safe little box. I praise Him for keeping me close and sustaining me through it all!

What's Abundant in Your Life?

"I am the Vine; you are the branches. Whoever lives in Me and I in him bears much (abundant) fruit. However, apart from Me [cut off from vital union with Me] you can do nothing." This wonderful verse found in John 15:5 of the Amplified Bible, Classic Edition, sums up many of our lives. I lived through those days of being able to "do nothing." I may have appeared busy or lazy, but nothing of value was being produced. No real rest was calming my soul. No amount of check marks on my to-do list made me satisfied for very long.

Have you been there? You work and you struggle and you look around at what's been accomplished. If you do it in your own effort, you feel super frustrated *a lot*. If you decide to pull yourself up by your boot straps, you can gloat for a while. Then, one mistake, and you're worse off and harder on yourself for feeling like a failure or disappointment. That's a vicious cycle with no good end.

Take a look at this verse again. In Christ, we bear "much (abundant) fruit." It's not a matter of maybe or hopefully, but it says ***whoever lives in Him bears much fruit***. If there's any question about what *living in Him* means, the Amplified Bible brings it out: *vital union* is critical. When you are alive in Christ, you have all you need to produce fruit. However, nothing grows when severed from the Vine.

We don't have many vineyards around North Mississippi or West Tennessee, but I've seen plenty of leaves falling in the autumn months. It didn't matter if they were from oaks, maples, dogwoods, beech, or apple trees. If a branch is off or a leaf detached, just give it a little time before it dries out and gets brittle. I've felt like a loose leaf before, crackly and dry, blown about by the wind and crumbling under pressure. Have you?

I don't claim to know a lot about the anatomy and physiology of our human bodies, but I know our *vital signs* are important. They are the first things an EMT checks at the scene of an accident. Your pulse, breathing, and body temperature will indicate life, or the loss of it. We cannot be fruitful if we aren't living *in Christ*. He must be our *vital necessity*, like our next breath and our heartbeat. If someone must have dialysis due to kidney problems, you wouldn't think they would skip it on days they don't feel like going to the clinic. It's *vital for life* that they go. Our longing for the presence of God should be this vital.

In *The Pursuit of God*, A.W. Tozer wrote:

> "I want deliberately to encourage this mighty longing after God. The lack of it has brought us to our present low estate. The stiff and wooden quality about our religious lives is a

result of our lack of holy desire. Complacency is a deadly foe of all spiritual growth. Acute desire must be present or there will be no manifestation of Christ to His people. He waits to be wanted. Too bad that with many of us He waits so long, so very long, in vain." ³

That last sentence is heart-wrenching. To know that our Creator longs for intimate fellowship, and us not be moved by that, is so sad, indeed.

With all this about the much, abundant fruit being said, I want to encourage you to look at the fruit of your life. What's being consumed, and what's being produced? Does the Fruit of the Spirit abound in your life—with bits of Love, Joy, Peace, Patience, Kindness, Goodness, Faithfulness, Gentleness, and Self-Control popping out in different sizes and variations? What do you long for? Is it eternal or temporal? Where do you invest your time, energy, and resources? Do you celebrate progress? How is your thought life? Do your words agree with what God says? These are questions we all go back to when maintaining balance in our daily lives.

Some Last(ing) Thoughts on Fruit

In the fall of 2015, I was called back for more tests after a mammogram. It was Breast Cancer Awareness Month, and I fought to keep my thoughts in check. I finally understood what so many people experience *while waiting*. Not knowing is such a hard place; I've had many opportunities along this journey to trust God with the details. There have been many things I've had to verbalize: "I can't understand this, Lord. But You know all things, and I trust You."

Those days of waiting for the biopsies and waiting for the calls—all the unknowns—tested and stretched me in new ways. I had been walking with the Lord and learning enough about my thoughts and words to know *where to begin*; I was careful with what I *allowed* myself *to think and say*. I held on to the Word of the Lord as He whispered to my heart. For weeks before I found out the results, and weeks after, Romans 8:28 kept popping up in random places. As we know, however, nothing is random with God.

An e-mail would show up in my inbox with that Bible verse. It would be in a morning devotional study. I'd look at my phone or the clock in the car and so many times: *8:28*. Every time, it built my faith. "And we know that all things work together for good to those who love God, to those who are the called according to *His* purpose." (Romans 8:28, NKJV) The results came back negative. Praise God! What a journey.

I still think about the dear ladies I met who were also having biopsies. A couple of us talked and shared some details. To one, I felt led to give the blue, palm-fitted cross stress reliever I had squeezed during my biopsy. It said *Trust in the Lord* on one side, and *Proverbs 3:5* on the other. I reassured her I never had to squeeze it for the pain; it wasn't that bad. Especially when you consider that having a child *is* painful. That made some of the fear fade from her face. (She had given birth three times—without epidurals.) Wherever you go and whoever you're around, you have the potential to increase and to offer your Good Fruit to many others. This blesses them, and it blesses you in the process. So often in life we can give away what we can't even do for ourselves; it's a great spiritual Truth that keeps us *connected to God* so *He* can work out the way *He* wants to take care of us. Here's a prime example: Need encouragement? Encourage someone else, and God will create an amazing way to give you encouragement.

My Main Squeeze

Finally, I want to end on this Good Fruit note concerning my husband. To describe the dysfunction of our failing marriage, I told the good, the bad, and the ugly about us. Being in a relationship with someone who is like you *or* someone who's opposite of you can be trying, to say the least. We heard Dr. Gary Chapman, author of *The 5 Love Languages*, at one of the marriage retreats a few years ago. After a couple of sessions, Kelly remarked, "We've been speaking different languages, but now I'm bilingual, baby!" Does that remind you of any of your relationships? What language have we been speaking, anyway?

Marriage can be the most difficult, yet the most rewarding, of any relationship. Trust me, ladies, you do *not* want your husband to complete you and make you first in his life. We often look to a person to make us happy or give us joy. This is not your husband's job either, ladies. He may have been really good at making himself number one for many years, just as you have been with yourself. You definitely need to be there for each other—with commitment and trust—to lift the one that is down at the moment, to see the best in your spouse, to encourage, respect, support, and cheer him on. You may not know it yet, or you may have discovered it years ago: *God is the One Who should complete you!* Only then can you truly love your man. It's only then that you'll find true joy and happiness. When you're his #2, and God is his #1, rest assured that you *will* be loved and taken care of.

Experience is speaking here, because I did it wrong for many years. It's still beautifully amazing every time my husband shows me grace when I *know* I've messed up. He could go on about it, making me feel bad for a while if he wanted to, but he moves on and never mentions it again. That's when I see Jesus in my husband. That's what I want others to see in me.

I felt led to begin a prayer journal about anything and everything a while back. I'll write some specific prayers and some in general. When God answers those prayers or moves in a special way, I'll jot it down with the date beside it. Kaleigh Brooke was thumbing through it one day, and saw a few pages titled *Things I Love About My Husband*. I had forgotten about it until she asked me what it was for. It was exactly what it said: descriptions about my husband's great qualities—from his generous heart to his blue eyes, from how he loves our daughter to his being a great provider for our family, and a lot more.

As I thought about the list, it made me smile. It's also good to mention now that I was fighting bad feelings toward him when I initially began it. There were two or three things I would become anxious about and allow to steal my joy. I would replay them in my mind and give them the spotlight. Focusing on the negatives will frustrate any effort to remember the great things we love about someone. This isn't just about positive thinking. It's about learning to make God the source of power behind our thoughts and words; then, we really see some good, abundant, lasting fruit.

Kelly and I still like to fish together when we get the chance. He baits the hook, lets me reel it in, and takes my catch off. He cleans the fish and cooks them better than any restaurant. We enjoy our time, and balance each other out. In areas where he's stronger, he leads with a sure hand. I encourage and honor him as a loyal wife and friend, and a good mother to his child. He gives me freedom to be me, and I do the same for him. On our own, we could go through life and follow God's calling. When we were born again and God restored our marriage, we began to learn an even better way. We are better together! Now, we can move forward and be fishers of men; God opens many doors of opportunity when we have willing hearts to be all that He created us to be.

The world needs to see the real struggles and the real saving grace behind godly marriages. There are enough things the enemy has taken and perverted; it's time we take our families back and fight this good fight of faith. Do you know what the Bible says about this? "And they overcame him by the blood of the Lamb, and by the word of their testimony; and they loved not their lives unto the death." (Revelation 12:11, KJV)

Jesus has already overcome death and the grave. It's by the blood of Jesus that we are now victorious. We must remember that *we have overcome* the evil one because the Lamb of God was *the perfect sacrifice* in our place. We must also remember we overcome by *speaking the praise and glory* due to God, telling what He has done for us—even in us and through us: "by the word of their testimony." <u>Some</u> on this planet will be called to give their lives as a martyr for their faith in Jesus Christ. <u>Many</u> will be called to do so in the boundaries of marriage, without actually dying (though it will often feel like you are when you put your spouse above your needs and wants).

When life gets bogged down and the season is long and tedious, remember that *you are an overcomer*! When the day has been long and daily life hits hard, I love to go outside and look up. The stars on a clear night take my breath away. It puts perspective on all the concerns and tasks of the day.

Huge things at work are dwarfed in the starlight. Family difficulties diminish when I see the milky spiral of our galaxy. Even clouds ushering in rain have a majestic presence as the wind escorts them along the horizon.

It reminds me of the story of our friend Abraham, whose faith journey we read about earlier. Before he had *any* evidence or saw *any* glimpse of God's promise being fulfilled, he believed. "Then the LORD took Abram outside and said to him, 'Look up into the sky and count the stars if you can. That's how many descendants you will have!' And Abram believed the LORD, and the LORD counted him as righteous because of his faith." (Genesis 15:5-6, NLT)

It's fantastic to think that God had Abram go out of his tent—away from looking at his surroundings and circumstances, away from that narrow perspective—and into the splendor of God's greatness. He simply needed to look up!

Life has many ways to drain us and compete for our time. Our relationships can pull us in many directions. Being offended must be addressed; staying offended should not be an option. Left to ourselves, we're nothing but a big mess.

We must stay *connected* to our Source. That is the key to our walk with the Lord. When you desire to know God and grow up in Him, you must make it a point to stay connected to Him. You need Him like you need your next heartbeat and your next breath. During the hopelessness of a pit, we may have discovered we were *desperate* for God. Now, we realize we're *desperate for Him* every second of every day. He will continue to usher *Hope* into our souls like a cool, bubbling brook in the heat of the day.

Let the Word of God get so rooted and grounded in your heart and soul that it becomes the Bread of Life sustaining you each day. Think of Jesus as your closest friend, and follow the promptings of the Holy Spirit within you. During the trials and valleys of life, remember the many things God has done for you; count your blessings and discover it's like counting the sand on a beach or the stars in the sky. Live with a heart of gratitude and thankfulness. Look up, and see a glimpse of just how big our God is! That will make for a fabulous life, flourishing with Fruit, and will ALWAYS lead to ***Something Wonderful***!

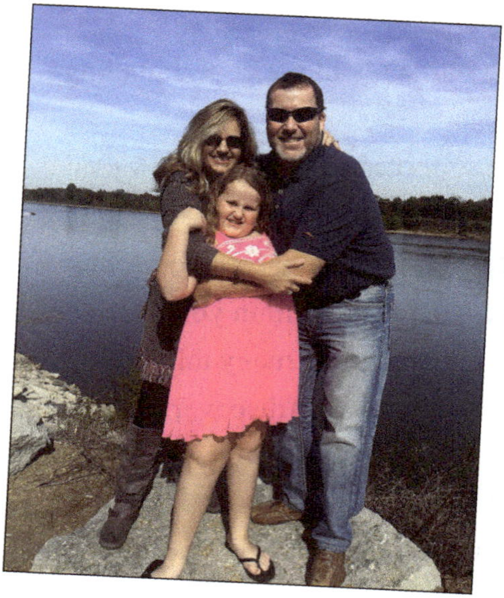

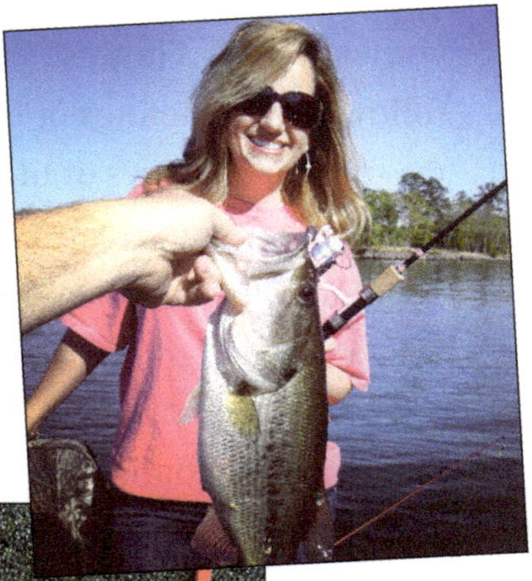

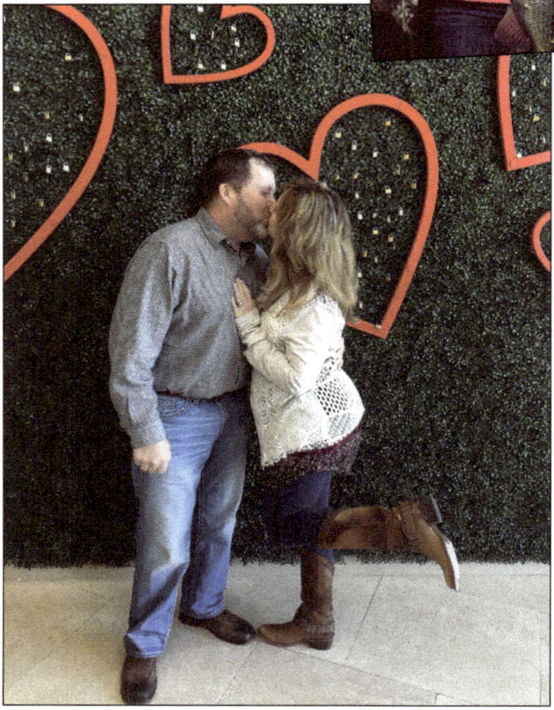

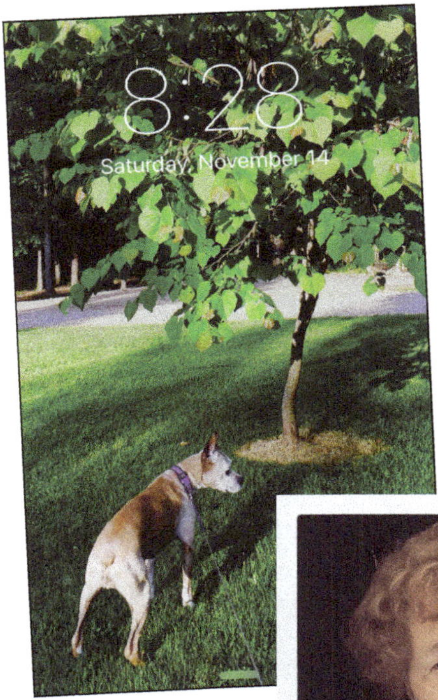
8:28
Saturday, November 14

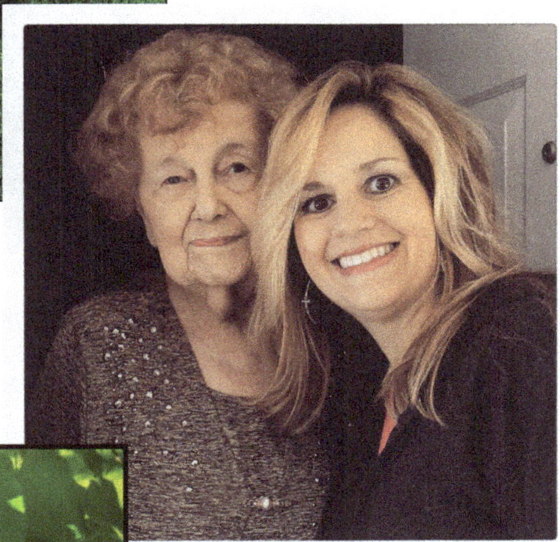

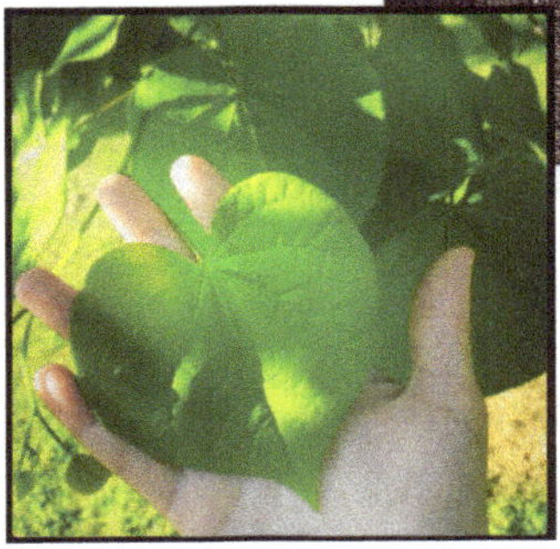

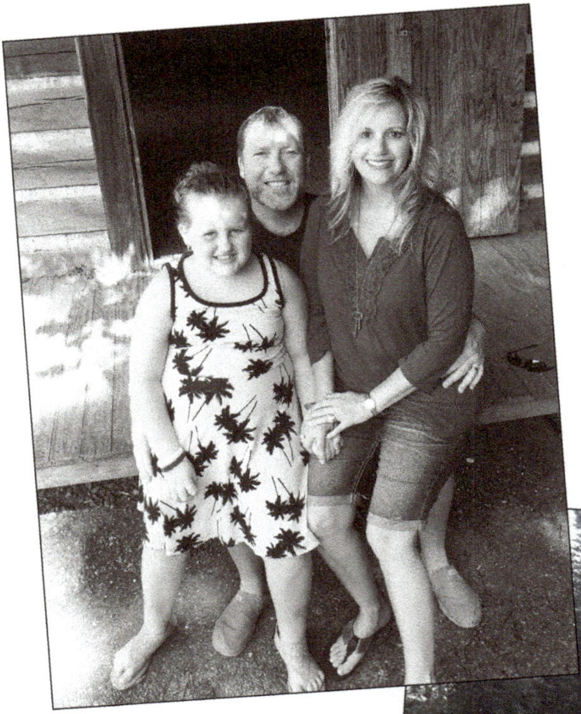

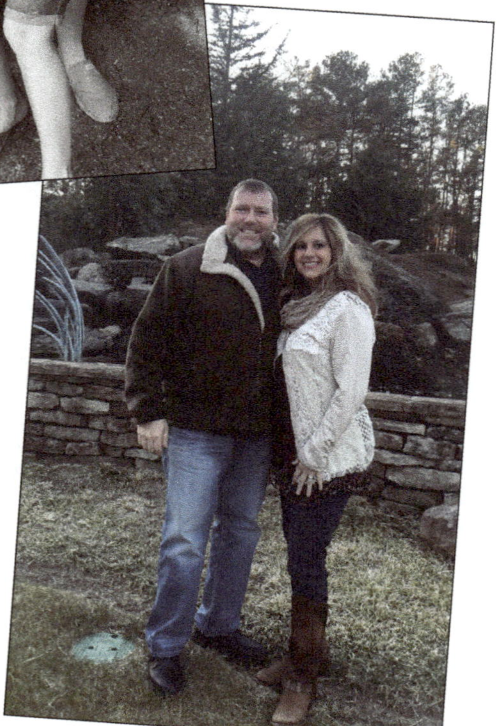

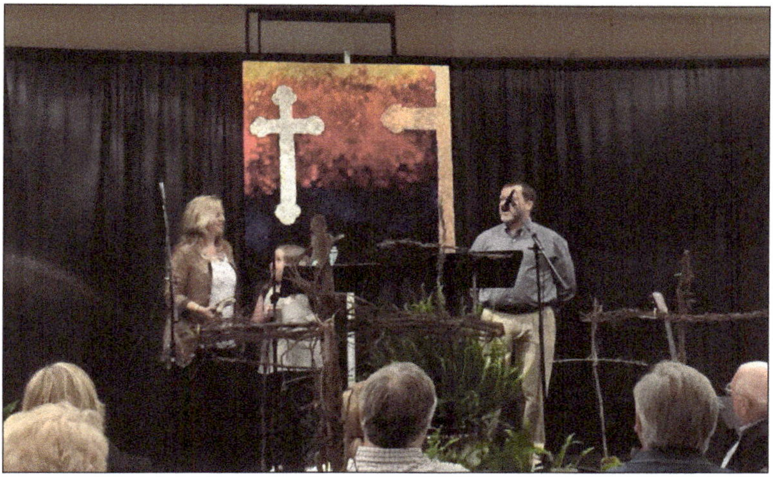

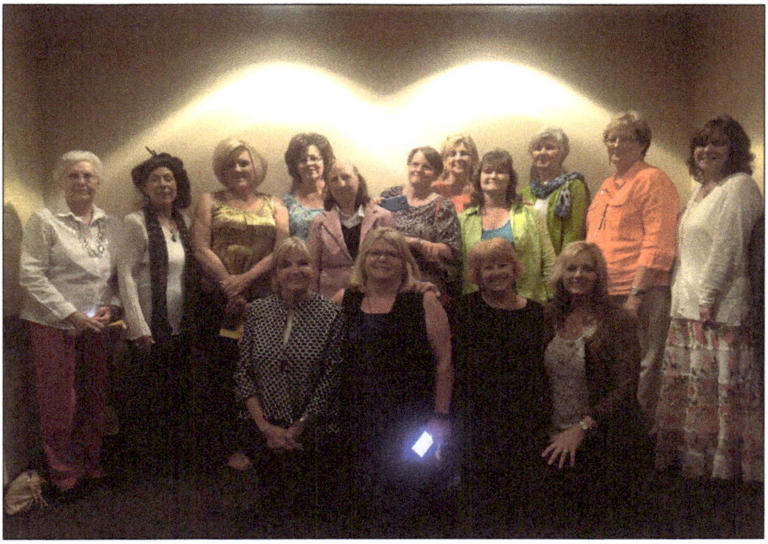

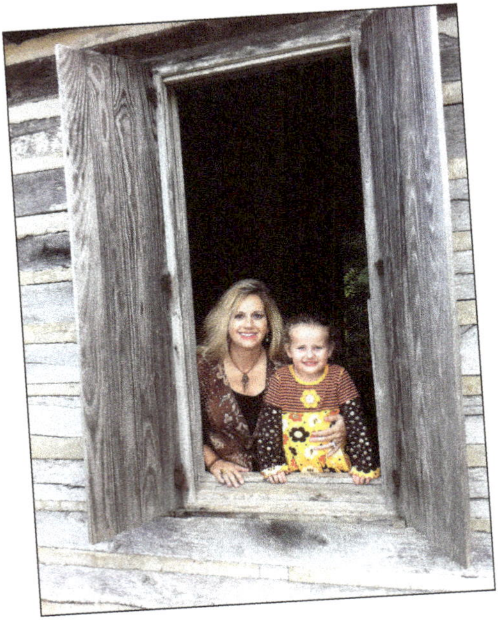

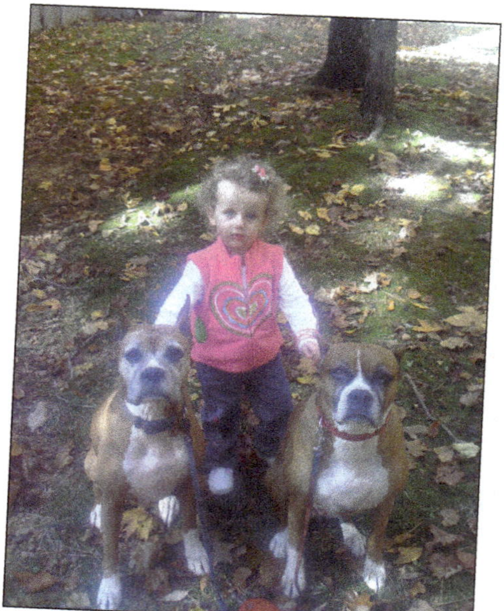

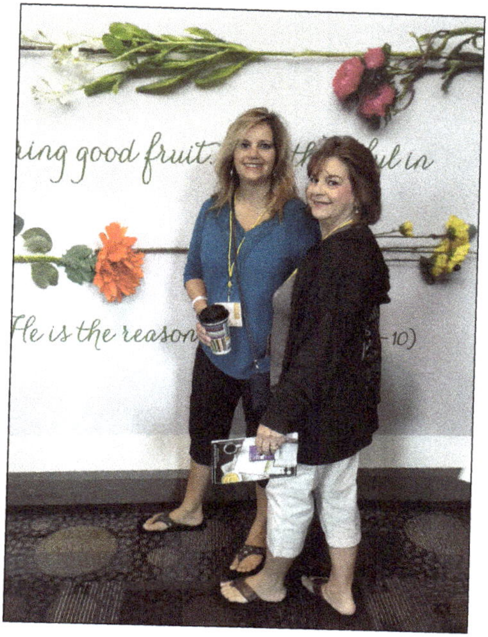
ring good fruit.
He is the reason

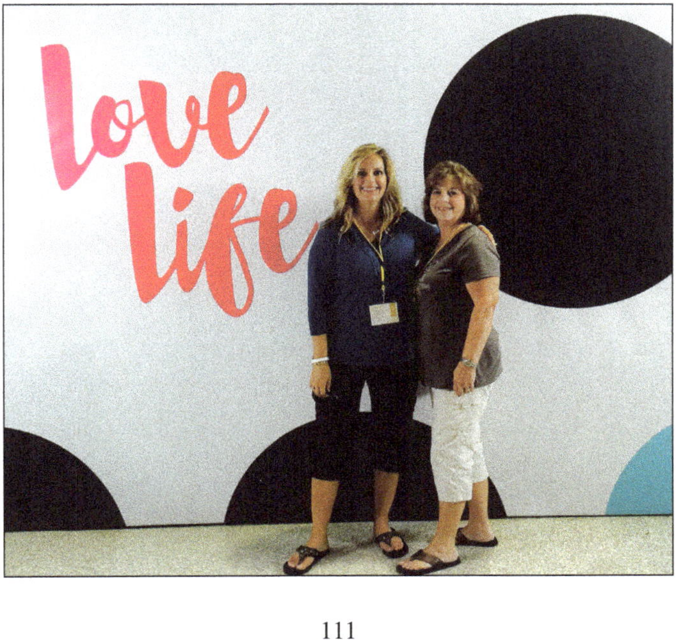
love
life

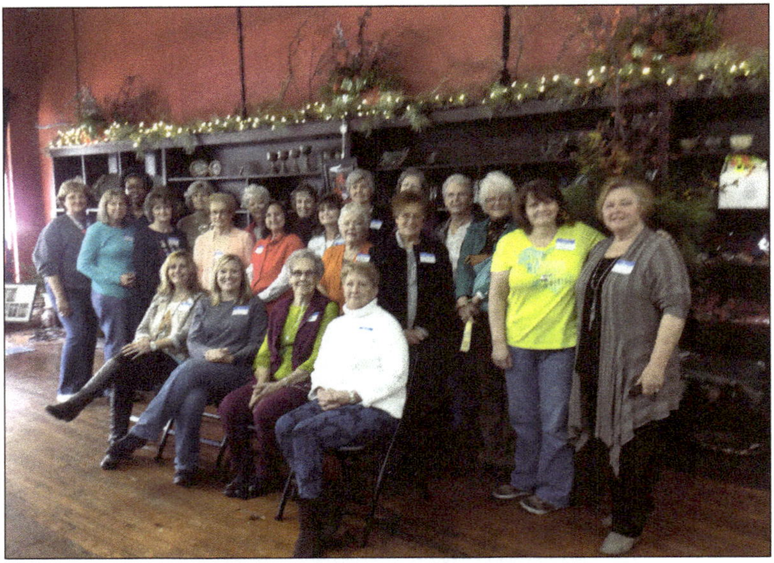

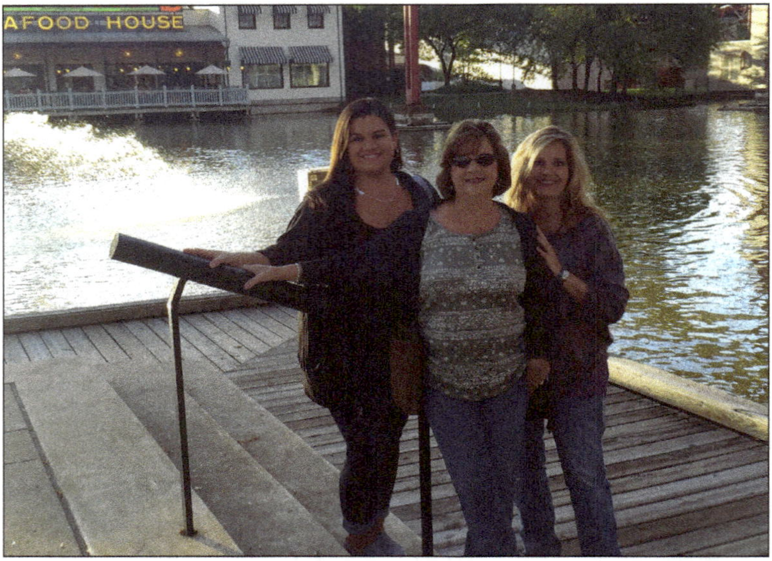
AFOOD HOUSE

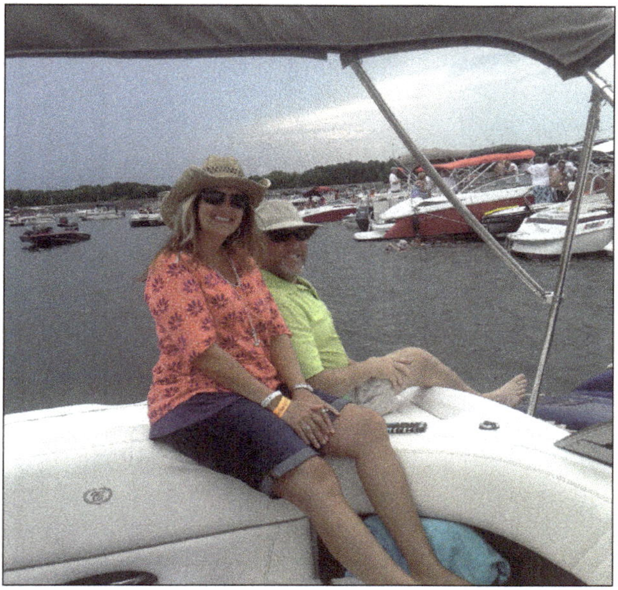

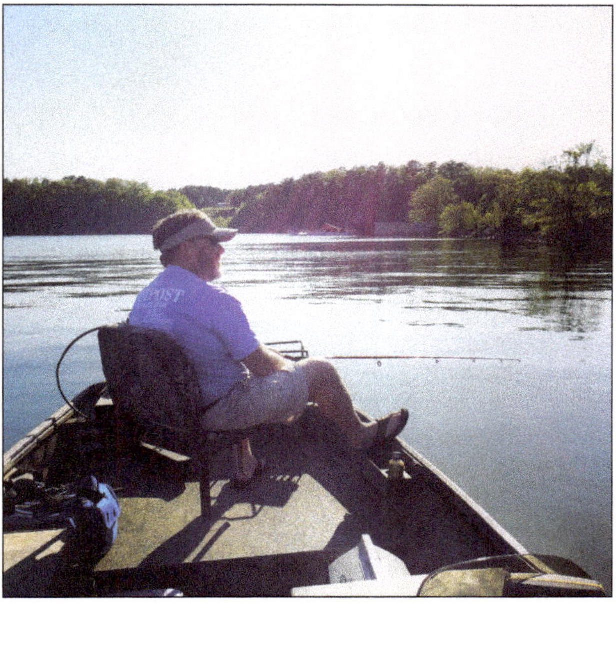

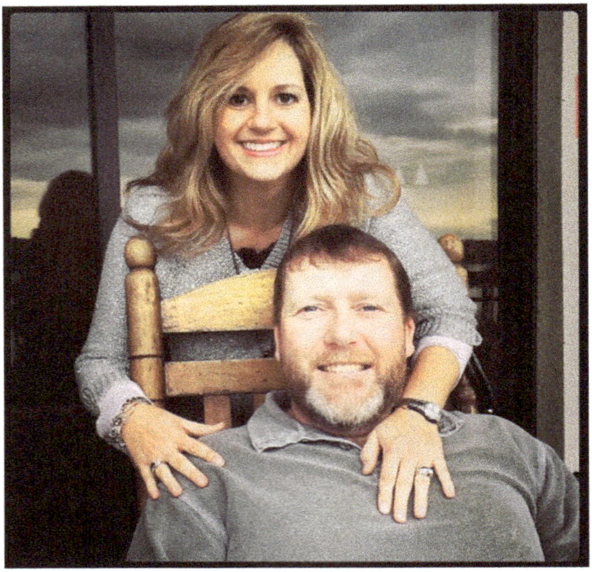

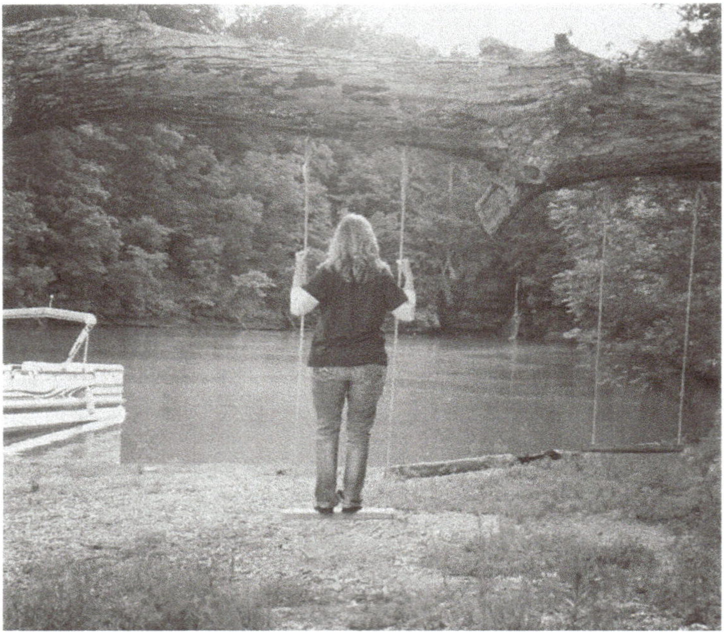

NOTES

[1] http://www.goodreads.com/quotes/23403-indeed-the-safest-road-to-hell-is-the-gradual-one—the

[2] 'Charismatic.' Encarta Dictionary: English (North America), Microsoft Office Word, 2007

[3] A.W. Tozer, The Pursuit of God (Camp Hill, PA: WingSpread Publishers, 2006), 17